W9-BQI-331

THE Living Universe

to Patricia & Peter,

With gratitude for your
courageous inquiries.

Warmest regards,

Diane.

9/10

Other books by Duane Elgin:

Voluntary Simplicity

Promise Ahead

Awakening Earth

Changing Images of Man (with Joseph Campbell and others)

Living Legacies (with Coleen LeDrew Elgin)

Duane Elgin

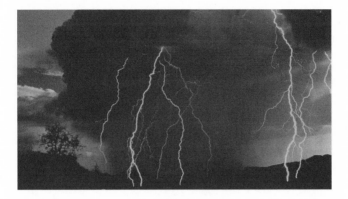

THE Living Universe

WHERE ARE WE? WHO ARE WE? WHERE ARE WE GOING?

FOREWORD BY DEEPAK CHOPRA

BK

Berrett–Koehler Publishers, Inc.
San Francisco
a BK Life book

Copyright © 2009 by Duane Elgin

All rights reserved. No part of this publication may be reproduced, distributed, or transmitted in any form or by any means, including photocopying, recording, or other electronic or mechanical methods, without the prior written permission of the publisher, except in the case of brief quotations embodied in critical reviews and certain other noncommercial uses permitted by copyright law. For permission requests, write to the publisher, addressed "Attention: Permissions Coordinator," at the address below.

Berrett-Koehler Publishers, Inc.
235 Montgomery Street, Suite 650
San Francisco, CA 94104-2916
Tel: (415) 288-0260   Fax: (415) 362-2512   www.bkconnection.com

Ordering Information

Quantity sales. Special discounts are available on quantity purchases by corporations, associations, and others. For details, contact the "Special Sales Department" at the Berrett-Koehler address above.

Individual sales. Berrett-Koehler publications are available through most bookstores. They can also be ordered directly from Berrett-Koehler: Tel: (800) 929-2929; Fax: (802) 864-7626; www.bkconnection.com

Orders for college textbook/course adoption use. Please contact Berrett-Koehler: Tel: (800) 929-2929; Fax: (802) 864-7626.

Orders by U.S. trade bookstores and wholesalers. Please contact Ingram Publisher Services, Tel: (800) 509-4887; Fax: (800) 838-1149; E-mail: customer.service@ingrampublisherservices.com; or visit www.ingrampublisherservices.com/Ordering for details about electronic ordering.

Berrett-Koehler and the BK logo are registered trademarks of Berrett-Koehler Publishers, Inc.

Printed in the United States of America

Berrett-Koehler books are printed on long-lasting acid-free paper. When it is available, we choose paper that has been manufactured by environmentally responsible processes. These may include using trees grown in sustainable forests, incorporating recycled paper, minimizing chlorine in bleaching, or recycling the energy produced at the paper mill.

Cataloging-in-Publication data is available from the Library of Congress.
ISBN 978-1-57675-969-1

First Edition
14 13 12 11 10 09   10 9 8 7 6 5 4 3 2 1

Book design and composition: Detta Penna
Copyeditor: Judith Johnstone
Illustrator: Camilla Coates
Proofreader: Katherine Lee
Indexer: Joan Dickey

Dedicated to the wisdom keepers
across cultures and through history
who guide our exploration
of the living universe.

Contents

Foreword

by Deepak Chopra

As a physician, I am concerned with healing. In my view, the more we are in touch with the universe we come from, the more we will be able to heal ourselves and at the same time heal our planet. We are an integral part of a living and intelligent universe. Not only is the universe alive, it is imbued with consciousness. The universe wants to live and breathe through you. To find out the truth of this, you need to relate to the universe as if it were alive. Otherwise, how will you ever know that it is? Today, begin to adopt the following habits:

Talk to the universe.
Listen for its reply.
Be on intimate terms with Nature.
See the life in everything.
Carry yourself like a child of the universe.

Duane Elgin writes about our living universe as an evolutionary pioneer. He has been an explorer of scientific knowledge and spiritual understanding for more than four decades. He has worked on a Presidential Commission looking into the deep future; helped pioneer sustainable ways of living with his book *Voluntary Simplicity*; developed a stunning view of the big picture of the human journey in *Awakening Earth*; co-founded three non-profit organizations working for media accountability and citizen empowerment, and more. The uniqueness and span of this book reflect Duane's wide-ranging life journey.

The Living Universe is written with elegant simplicity and yet it addresses our most important existential dilemmas.

Where are we? Who are we? What journey are we on? Step-by-step he offers us new insights about ourselves and our human journey. At the foundation is the understanding that we are each an expression of a living universe. The universe is conscious, self-regulating, self-creating, ever-renewing, and always evolving to increasing levels of complexity and creativity.

Through us (the human nervous system), the universe is becoming increasingly aware of itself. We are beings of light, love, music, and happiness. We are evolving toward unity consciousness where we experience ourselves as cosmic beings participating in the evolution of the universe. If we consciously participate in this evolutionary process, we can heal the rift in our collective soul and bring creative solutions to poverty, social injustice, war, terrorism, and ecological devastation. If we ignore the call to our collective awakening, we put at risk the future of human civilization on our precious planet. The choice is ours.

It is my hope that the human family rapidly awakens itself to the reality that we live in a living universe. The human body is part of the cosmic body. The human mind is part of the cosmic mind. Awakening to this cosmic dimension of ourselves is profoundly restorative. With that experience and understanding, we bring healing to our wounded planet and a new sense of adventure to the human journey.

Duane has written an important book because, at this pivotal time when we are separated by so many differences, it is vital that we discover our common ground as a species. A widely shared understanding that we all live in the same living universe provides the foundation for positive visions of the future that offer beacons of hope to pierce the darkness of the world's gathering storms.

Preface

As I complete this book in early 2009, a number of crises are putting the world system under enormous pressure to make fundamental changes: economic breakdowns, growing climate disruption, the end of cheap oil, desperate poverty, violent conflicts over resources and religion, the proliferation of weapons of mass destruction, and more. We are fulfilling the "Warning to Humanity" given by more than 1,600 of the world's senior scientists, including a majority of the Nobel laureates in the sciences.[1] In 1992 they warned: "A great change in our stewardship of the earth and the life on it is required, if vast human misery is to be avoided and our global home on this planet is not to be irretrievably mutilated." If a "great change" in our stewardship of life is essential, what does that change look like? Given the enormous differences and divisions within the human community, where can we find a commonly shared understanding for building a new pathway into the future?

To align our efforts and fulfill our potentials, it is vital for the human family to find a compelling sense of direction for living and growing together. But what vision of humanity's journey has the breadth, depth, and reach to enable us to look beyond our many differences and galvanize our efforts in building a promising future? This integrative vision, or "great story," of humanity's journey can be summarized as follows: *The universe is deeply alive as an evolving and learning system and we humans are on a journey of discovery within it. We are learning to live within a living universe.* If we lose sight of *where we are* (living in a living universe) we profoundly diminish our understanding of *who we are* (beings of both biological and cosmic dimension) and *where we are going* (growing into an ever more intimate relationship with the living universe).

We cannot understand who we are or the journey we are on without first understanding where we are and the universe we are in. Our future pivots on how we answer the question of whether we regard the universe as dead or alive. As we will explore in great detail throughout this book, I think the evidence points toward regarding the universe as alive. We will progressively unfold what this means, but here is a preliminary distinction between these two views:

Dead universe view. The universe is a barren and inhospitable place comprised almost entirely of non-living matter and empty space. Life is extremely rare. On Earth, matter has somehow organized itself to high levels of complexity and has produced living entities. However, considered in the context of the larger universe, the human enterprise is a trivial speck. Our existence as humans appears to be pointless and without purpose—a cosmic accident that will be forgotten. A dead universe has no memory and tells no stories. When the body dies, the "lights go out" and we disperse, leaving no trace or remnant, either physical or non-physical. What matters most is matter—material possessions, material power, material pleasure, and material prestige.

Living universe view. In counterpoint to the dead universe perspective, the living universe is a paradigm that portrays the universe as buzzing with invisible energy and aliveness, patiently growing a garden of cosmic scale. It suggests that we humans, as conscious life forms in this immensity, are very precious. We serve an important purpose for a universe growing conscious forms of life: Through us, the universe sees, knows, feels, and learns. We are learning how to live ever more consciously in a living universe. What matters most is not matter but what is invisible—the aliveness within ourselves, our relationships, and the world around us.

Several hundred years ago, the mechanistic and materialistic view of a non-living universe was liberating—part of the Enlightenment-born rationalism that helped humanity free itself from superstition and fear to achieve extraordinary intellectual and technological breakthroughs. But this paradigm no longer serves human evolution. By removing aliveness from the fabric of the universe, the initial success of the materialistic perspective has ultimately led to environmental exploitation and a profound global crisis.

Because our view of the universe creates the context within which we understand and choose our future, it is critically important that we have an accurate understanding of our cosmic home. Where a dead-universe perspective generates alienation and despair, a living-universe perspective generates inspiring and resilient visions of a higher pathway for humanity. Is this affirming view of the future justified?

Three core questions run through this book. The Introduction sets the stage and focuses the inquiry. We explore the first question—*Where are we?*—in the next two chapters. In Chapter 1, we expand our thinking about the universe and ourselves. In Chapter 2, we consider the universe through the lens of science and ask whether it has the basic characteristics of a living entity. Because the science of life is at an early stage, it is premature to declare that science can prove the universe is a living system. Instead we ask, does this evidence *point in the direction* of a living or a non-living universe? If so, how does this matter?

We then explore the second question—*Who are we?*—in Chapters 3, 4, and 5. In Chapter 3, we explore who we are in relation to the universe through the eyes of the world's major religious and wisdom traditions. In Chapter 4, we consider how a "Mother Universe" can contain countless daughter universes, including our own. Chapter 5 explores our soulful nature as cosmic beings learning to live in a living universe.

We explore the third question—*Where are we going?*—in Chapters 6 and 7. In Chapter 6, we ask where is the universe going? Does it have an evolutionary direction that is apparent? If so, how does our journey fit with it? Are we "going with the flow," or not? In Chapter 7, we look at where we are on our journey and focus on the unprecedented pivot we are making as a species—moving from a path of separation and differentiation to a path of connection and communion.

In closing, Chapter 8 presents six tasks that are vital for our journey home and Chapter 9 offers suggestions for personal meditation and group conversation that explore the theme of a living universe.

Acknowledgments

I am grateful for the support of the many people whose unique contributions helped bring this book into the world. First, I appreciate those who, through their financial support, enabled me to complete this lifetime project. I especially want to acknowledge two individuals who were initial supporters, Ted Mallon and John Levy; thank you for your trust in me and in this work. Three foundations stepped forward with important grants: the Kalliopeia Foundation in California (thank you, Barbara Sargent and Barbara Cushing), the Fetzer Institute in Michigan (thank you, Frances Vaughan), and the Foundation for Global Community in California (thank you, Richard Rathbun). I am grateful to other individuals who provided important support along the way: Kimberly and Foster Gamble, John Steiner and Margo King, and Charles Silverstein. The president of the RSF SocialFinance organization, Mark Finser, was an invaluable ally who provided a fiscal home for the living universe project.

Second, I want to express my great appreciation to those whose feedback helped to shape this work. Deepak Chopra, I am deeply grateful for your Foreword. Profound thanks also to the community of friends and scholars who critiqued earlier versions of this book: Chris Bache, Bill Barnard, Coleen LeDrew Elgin, Dave Ellis, Scott Elrod, Kimberly and Foster Gamble, Roger Housden, Jean Houston, John Levy, Joel Levey, Nipun Mehta, Carter Phipps, Frank Poletti, Richard Rathbun, Charles Silverstein, Bill Veltrop, and Roger Walsh. Your feedback was invaluable in moving the work toward its greatest potential. I am also grateful to Colleen Mauro for her expert editing of the initial draft.

Third, my great appreciation goes to the superb publishing team at Berrett-Koehler, who were so helpful, transparent, and professional throughout the publishing process. I especially want to acknowledge Steve Piersanti for his skilled collaboration as my editor and his creative leadership as president of Berrett-Koehler. Steve's feedback was restrained, persistent, discerning, and consistently helpful. I am grateful for the support of Judy Johnstone and her skillful editing of the final manuscript. To Detta Penna, many thanks for her elegant design and for seeing this project through production. To Camilla Coates, my grateful thanks for her graceful illustrations. I also appreciated the editorial feedback of B-K authors Alan Briskin, Dee Hock, David Korten, and Libba Pinchot, and B-K manuscript reviewers Douglas Dupler, Elainne Obadia, John Renesch, and Don Schatz.

Finally, I want to express my great appreciation to my wife Coleen LeDrew Elgin for her feedback on this manuscript and for being such a loving and supportive partner as, together, we learn to live in the living universe.

Duane Elgin
February, 2009

The Great Awakening

The universe is a communion and a community.
We ourselves are that communion become conscious of itself.
—Thomas Berry[1]

Is the universe non-living at its foundations? If it is dead and without consciousness in its underpinnings, then it is unaware of—and indifferent to—our existence. What do you think? Are we strangers in a strange land, unwelcome outsiders?

What if, instead, the universe is alive at its deepest foundations? If there is a permeating field of aliveness and an ecology of consciousness throughout the universe, what does that mean for our life and life purpose?

You may wonder, with the challenges of climate disruption, energy shortages, wars over resources, deep poverty, and more, why should you care about the universe and our connection with it? My answer is that we humans need to step back and get our bearings.

The dream of material prosperity is becoming a collective nightmare as we overwhelm the Earth with our sheer numbers and our voracious appetites as consumers. With growing urgency we are being pushed to imagine new ways we can live together agreeably and sustainably on this planet. Yet we find ourselves without a compelling sense of direction. It feels as if we are wandering into history—alienated from the Earth, from one another, and from the universe. We are lost. Where do we find a way forward that articulates a common journey for the human family?

I believe we must look beyond devising solutions to the energy crisis or the climate crisis, although that is important. Possibly the most fundamental challenge facing humanity is to look beyond adversity and visualize futures of great opportunity. In a self-fulfilling prophecy, we actualize who we think we are. The archetypes and stories we present to ourselves act as beacons guiding us into the future. To explore potential guiding images, let us step back, draw upon the deepest wisdom that humanity has to offer, and ask three fundamental questions:

1. **Where are we?** Although there is a natural inclination to start with ourselves, it is important to begin with the question of where we are rather than who we are. When we start with ourselves, we tend to asssume that our physical body defines who we are, and from this a cascade of consequences flow—giving us the kind of world we have now. If we begin, not with ourselves, but with *where* we are, and if we freshly open to the universe and ask what kind of place this is, then we may be led to a larger understanding; we may see that we are more than biological beings—that we have a cosmic connection as well.

Let's look at the universe in which we live and ask this core question: Do we live in a living or non-living universe? Einstein said if he could ask God one question, it would be "Is the universe friendly or not?" This book asks an even deeper question: Is the universe *alive* or not? The way we answer this simple question has profound implications for whether we experience life with feelings of alienation or belonging, see it as pointless or purposeful, and regard it with feelings of indifference or reverence.

2. **Who are we?** Having looked at the universe in which we live, we can now ask: Are we beings limited to our physical biology or do we somehow participate intimately with the larger universe? Our collective self-image as a species has yet to form, but it will emerge vividly within the next few decades as the communications revolution intersects with the perfect storm of an unyielding, whole-systems crisis for the Earth. This unfolding crisis will force us to take a hard look at ourselves in the mirror of our collective media and ask "Who are we as a species?" Are we no more than bio-physical beings in a struggle for material survival—or do we have a cosmic connection and purpose that calls us to awaken to a vastly larger potential?

3. **Where are we going?** Is there a discernible direction to life and evolution? Without a dramatic change in direction, humanity is headed toward catastrophe. The changes required for humanity to live sustainably on the Earth are so broad, so deep, and so far-reaching that if we are to avoid a global calamity it is crucial that we discover "great stories" that can align and orient our journey into the future. Is there a story of our awakening as a species with such compelling promise that it overcomes our fears and our historical inertia?

A Personal Perspective

To bring a more personal perspective to these questions, I want to share a few experiences that have been important threads in the tapestry of my life. Connecting with the miracle of aliveness has been a passionate interest since growing up on an Idaho farm in the 1940s and 1950s. I was born prematurely to my mother, a nurse, and my father, a farmer. We lived in the country with my brother, two dogs, a half-dozen cats and assorted farm animals a couple of miles outside of a small town of about five hundred people. Growing up in the big sky country of Idaho, I felt myself a small creature against a vast landscape. Because I worked on the farm until my early twenties, my roots are in the land, and I feel as much a sense of identity as a farmer as I do a scholar, educator, or activist.

Some of my earliest recollections are of lying on the living room floor and watching sunbeams pouring through a window and moving across the rug, their golden rays bringing a living presence and nurturing aliveness into the room. As a young man, farm life brought me the gift of deep silence in a setting where subtle ecstasies would regularly blossom: the smell of freshly mown hay, the fragrance of dry earth moistened by a brief summer shower, the Sun setting over distant mountains. When alone, I would sometimes lie down in a furrow to experience the earth and the sea of flourishing crops. I recall lying down in a field of lettuce, nearly covered by its abundant leaves, and absorbing the humming aliveness of the earth, the fields, and the sky above me. Irrigating crops, pruning apple trees, tending farm animals — these were regular invitations to celebrate nature's miracle of luminous aliveness. Like water seeping into a dry sponge, over many seasons a nameless and palpable presence gradually permeated me.

In my early twenties I moved to the city, where I felt a deep separation from the familiar aliveness of my farming days. In 1971, I was working in Washington, D.C., as a senior staff member of a joint presidential-congressional commission on the American future. Thoughts about the aliveness of nature were set aside as we focused on the next thirty years and issues of population growth, urbanization, and the shortage of critical resources like water. Although intuitions of a living universe still resonated within me, in the intense world of politics they seemed a soft sensibility to be disregarded. Still, I was conflicted. Was the living presence I experienced on the farm in Idaho just my imagination? Or, did the invisible aliveness permeate even the coarse world of Washington politics? How important was something so hard to grasp and yet so rich with felt experience?

After two years in Washington and disillusioned with the politics of power, I wanted a fresh start. With my family I moved to the San Francisco Bay Area and began to work with a small team of senior researchers in the "futures group" of SRI International, one of the largest think tanks in the world. For the next five years, we studied the long-range future for both government agencies and corporations. During this time I co-authored the book *Changing Images of Man* with a small team that included the eminent scholar Joseph Campbell. Our research explored archetypal images that serve as beacons to guide the human family into the future. Another project involved a yearlong study of future global problems for the president's science advisor. Still another project for the Environmental Protection Agency involved looking ahead twenty-five years and projecting an array of alternative scenarios and their implications for U.S. environmental policy. All of this research led me to the stark realization that our world is moving into a time of profound change in the ways we live on the Earth and see the universe, ourselves, and the human journey.

While engaged in researching the long-range future, I was also involved in an intense meditation practice grounded in Tibetan Buddhism. Then, in an unexpected turn of events, I became a subject in the earliest psychic research at SRI on behalf of the National Aeronautics and Space Administration. These scientific experiments gave me a way to explore over a period of nearly three years, in my direct experience, the fundamental question raised here: Is the universe a living system? Combining intensive meditation with equally intensive laboratory experimentation gave me an unusual learning opportunity. This book is grounded in the confidence of these years of combined inner and outer inquiry.

The SRI research on the global future made it emphatically clear that the world would soon encounter unyielding limits to current levels and patterns of growth. Seeing this, I wanted to do more than watch from the sidelines of history, so I left SRI in order to meditate and advocate for creative change.

Meditation took the form of a half-year of self-directed reflection and contemplation in my cottage. This culminated in a transformative experience that has reverberated through my life ever since (described in my book *Awakening Earth*, Appendix II). Insights from this half-year of meditation are reflected throughout this book.

My advocacy for change has included writing three editions of the book *Voluntary Simplicity* and speaking around the world on themes of building a sustainable future. I've also co-founded three non-profit organizations doing non-partisan work for media accountability and citizen empowerment.

Looking back, these diverse life experiences have given me a range of perspectives for looking at the world. So far, I have lived in at least three different perceptual paradigms. I grew up in the mindset of the agrarian era—on a farm where the experience of life was dominated by the seasons and cycles of nature. I then moved into the mindset of the industrial era as I watched our family farm grow into a small agribusiness and we moved from the farm into a nearby town. I then moved into the mindset of the communications era when I began doing research on long-range futures and advocating for a more conscious democracy. I've seen how each paradigm develops logically from the last, and each has its unique way of regarding the world and one's self.

Like myself, I believe many people may be living with a foot in at least two worlds: straddling two or more different paradigms of perception and struggling to make sense of the universe. Perhaps you, like me, feel pulled between opening with vulnerability to the subtle aliveness of the natural world and protecting your experience of aliveness from the deadness of a materially obsessed culture.

Before exploring the idea of a living universe, it is important to acknowledge its antithesis—an extreme view that regards the universe as non-living or dead at its foundations. I believe that seeing the universe as mostly dead matter, empty space, and devoid of life represents an important stage in humanity's individuation and empowerment. I also believe this is not the whole story, just one chapter in a much larger story of our awakening—and eventual return—to a living universe.

Living in a Dead Universe

For perspective, it is important to look carefully at the perceptual paradigm of a dead universe. Particularly in the world of science, it is not uncommon to encounter the view that we live in a universe that, at its foundation, lacks feeling, consciousness, and vitality. This view is clearly expressed, for example, by Susan Blackmore, an author on human consciousness, who said: "We live in a pointless universe. We're here for no reason at all. There isn't a soul. There isn't a spirit. We're not going to live forever in some kind of heaven

. . . there are no paranormal phenomena, although I can't be sure of that."[2]

Blackmore provides a stark description of a non-living or dead universe—and she is not alone.[3] This has been the established view of many scientists for three centuries. For more than 300 years, science has viewed the physical universe as "all there is": all that exists are various combinations of inert matter and to suggest otherwise is to regress into superstition. Matter, at the atomic level, is assumed to lack any kind of inherent vitality. In turn, aliveness, thought, and feelings are phenomena that mysteriously arise when matter evolves to high levels of complexity in its physical organization and creates beings like ourselves. All of existence is explained solely in material terms (except for the part about life spontaneously organizing itself and becoming conscious of itself). There appears to be no need for an invisible consciousness because the workings of the entire universe are explained through the workings of matter. Because human aliveness, thought, and feeling are assumed to have emerged from chemical reactions between non-living matter, the death of the physical body is seen as the end of consciousness. Understandably, in this view of the universe, more "basic" forms of matter (atoms and molecules) are thought to have no vitality or consciousness of any kind.

If the foundations of the universe are regarded as non-living, then "life" seems to have emerged only recently as matter somehow managed to organize itself into ever-higher levels of complexity—evolving from atoms to molecules to cells to organisms. Consciousness, or a knowing capacity, is viewed as a biological phenomena located in the physical brain.

If we assume the universe is non-living and without sentience at its foundations, it is natural to further assume there is no higher purpose or meaning to life. Love and happiness are no more than chemical reactions in the body and have no other meaning or significance. There is no prospect of a future beyond our physical existence. Because the universe will disperse and the stars burn out, all life will eventually die off and be forgotten, meaning nothing. Material possessions and accomplishments are the primary expression of one's identity, and thus an important source of happiness.

In this matter-only view of the universe, it is only logical to conclude that the most intensely living (we humans) have the right to exploit that which is dead (matter and the rest of nature) for our own purposes. Nature is our warehouse, filled with resources for our use. How should we relate to the world? By exploiting that which is dead (nature) on behalf of the living (ourselves). A tendency toward materialism, hedonism, and the exploitation of nature are predictable outcomes from a dead-universe perspective.

Despite its bleak outlook, a dead-universe perspective represents a critically important stage in humanity's long journey of awakening. In pulling back from nature and pulling apart from one another, we have also become much stronger and more differentiated as individuals. My sense is that we humans have separated ourselves as far from union with nature as we will ever go. Now we have little choice: If we are to continue to evolve and realize our potentials as a species, we *must* become conscious of our partnership with nature and one another.

Although the transition to industrial society and hyper-rationalism have largely severed it, I believe we are opening to a new level of connection with nature, particularly in science. From the electron microscope to the Hubble telescope to the human genome, we are transforming how we look at and understand the universe and ourselves. The more we look, the more we are finding the universe to be a place of breathtaking immensity, astonishing subtlety, and unfathomable mystery.

Cosmophilia: Love of the Universe

The term *biophilia* was first used by Erich Fromm to describe a psychological connection and sense of affiliation between humans and other forms of life. The eminent biologist, E. O. Wilson, has popularized this term and used it to describe our innate urge to affiliate with other living things. In feeling a sense of kinship and connection with other forms of life, we take a quantum leap forward in our motivation to care for all living things.

We can expand this feeling of connection and appreciation of life to the entire *cosmos*—a word that was first used by the Greek philosopher Pythagoras to describe our universe as a living embodiment of nature's order, harmony, and beauty. Building upon the concept of biophilia, we can create the word *cosmophilia*. Cosmophilia describes the kinship and affiliation we feel with the totality of nature and our experience of felt connection with the harmony and beauty of our universe. Our relationship with the universe involves both biophilia (love of other living things) and cosmophilia (love of the universe in its wholeness).

Naturalists have looked deeply into the nature of the universe and have come away in awe of her beauty and aliveness:

> Climb the mountains and get their good tidings. Nature's peace
> will flow into you as sunshine flows into trees. The winds will
> blow their own freshness into you, and the storms their energy,
> while cares will drop off like autumn leaves.
>
> —JOHN MUIR, EXPLORER AND NATURALIST

I believe in God, only I spell it Nature.

— Frank Lloyd Wright, architect

A feeling of profound and intimate connection with nature and the universe is a theme that emerges from reflections by astronauts:

> On the return trip home, gazing through 240,000 miles of
> space toward the stars and the planet from which I had come,
> I suddenly experienced the Universe as intelligent, loving,
> harmonious.

— Edgar Mitchell

> When I was the last man to walk on the moon in December
> 1972, I stood in the blue darkness and looked in awe at the Earth
> from the lunar surface. What I saw was almost too beautiful to
> grasp. There was too much logic, too much purpose—it was just
> too beautiful to have happened by accident.

— Gene Cernan

There is a vivid feeling of connection and communion that we can experience with nature at every scale—from a small flower to a galaxy. With cosmophilia, we feel our direct immersion in the subtle field of aliveness and energy that permeates the universe.

That we live in a living field of existence is an ancient insight. Only in the last few hundred years has science disengaged the modern mind from this view by asserting that matter is lifeless and space is but an empty stage. Now the tools of science are bringing into question the assumption of a non-living universe. Just as we are beginning to consider whether the Earth is a unified, living organism, we are also beginning to ask whether the universe is a single, integrated, life-form. The meaning of the phrase is complex, but a useful definition is that *a living universe is a unified and completely interdependent system that is continuously regenerated by the flow-through of phenomenal amounts of life energy whose essential nature includes consciousness or a self-reflective capacity that enables systems at every scale of existence to exercise some freedom of choice.* We will consider all of these characteristics and more in Chapter 2.

Does Aliveness Make a Difference?

What difference does it make if the universe is dead or alive? When children are starving, climate is destabilizing, oil is dwindling, and population is growing, why is it important to put our attention there? So what if we live in a living universe—why should that matter? Below are a few of the core reasons why it makes a profound difference whether we regard the universe as dead or alive. I'll present these polarities in stark terms to make the contrasts clear.

Is the universe indifferent or welcoming? How we feel about the surrounding universe has an enormous impact on our experience of life. If we think of the universe as dead at the foundations, then feelings of existential alienation, anxiety, dread, and fear are understandable. Why seek communion with the cold indifference of lifeless matter and empty space? If we relax into life, we will simply sink into existential despair. However, if we live in a living universe, feelings of subtle connection, curiosity, and gratitude are understandable. We see ourselves as participants in a cosmic garden of life that the universe has been patiently nurturing over billions of years. A living-universe perspective invites us to shift from indifference, fear, and cynicism to curiosity, love, and awe.

Are we forgotten or remembered? A non-living universe is without consciousness at its foundations so it is indifferent to humanity and our evolving creations. Nothing we do will ultimately matter. All will be forgotten. A dead universe has no deeper purpose or meaning. It does not matter whether it is a person or an entire world civilization, the same principle applies: a dead universe tells no stories. A living universe is itself a vast story continuously unfolding with countless unique characters playing out gripping dramas of awakening. The essence of these stories and the learning from them is remembered and conserved so that an evolving universe has wisdom to pass along to her offspring.

Pull apart or pull together? If we see the universe as mostly barren and devoid of life and our time on Earth as primarily a struggle for material existence, then it makes sense that we humans would pull apart in conflict. However, if we see the universe as intensely alive and our time on Earth as a journey of discovery into that aliveness, then it makes sense that we would pull together in cooperation in order to realize this magnificent potential.

Consumerism or conscious simplicity? Materialism is a rational response to living in a dead universe. In a material universe, consumerism offers a source of identity and a measure of significance and accomplishment. Where do I find pleasure in a non-living universe? In things. How do I know that I amount to anything? By how much stuff I have accumulated. How should I relate to the world? By exploiting that which is dead (the universe) on behalf of the living (myself). Consumerism and exploitation are natural outcomes of a dead-universe perspective. However, if we view the foundations of the universe as being intensely alive, then it makes sense to minimize the material clutter and needless busyness and grow in the non-material riches of life—nurturing relationships, caring communities, creative expressions, and more.

Are we separate or inter-connected? If we are no more than biological entities and we are fundamentally separate from one another, then it makes sense to see ourselves as disconnected from the suffering of other living beings. However, if we are all swimming in the same ocean of subtle aliveness, then it makes sense that we would each have a direct experience of communion with, and concern for, the well-being of others. If we share the same matrix of existence, then the rest of life is already touching me, co-creating the field within which I exist.

Who and what are we? Are we no more than a collection of elements that are experiencing a series of chemical and neurological reactions? Is there more to ourselves than our material-biological components? In a dead universe, the boundaries of our being are defined by the extent of our physical body. However, in a living universe, our physical existence is permeated and sustained by an aliveness that is inseparable from the aliveness of the universe. If we are beings whose consciousness can extend beyond our biological bodies and into the reaches of the living universe, then our physical bodies comprise only the smallest fraction of the full scope of our being.

These are just a few of the fundamental ways that our approach to life can be radically different depending on which of these two perspectives seem most real. Everyday life, of course, is not so clear-cut as these polarities suggest. The important point is that, whether we regard the universe as dead or alive at its foundations has enormous consequences for our future, both individually and collectively.

Overall, I do not believe that the human community can come to a new relationship with one another and the Earth unless we also come to a new relationship with the universe. Life-changing consequences flow from this new perspective.

Part One

Where Are We?

Chapter 1

The First Miracle

Nature is incomprehensible at first,
Be not discouraged, keep on,
There are divine things well envelop'd,
I swear to you there are divine beings
More beautiful than words can tell.

—WALT WHITMAN[1]

American Indian lore speaks of three miracles. The first miracle is that anything exists at all. The second miracle is that living things exist. The third miracle is that living things exist that *know* they exist. As human beings conscious of ourselves, we represent the third miracle.[2]

In celebrating ourselves, it is important that we not overlook the first miracle: the natural world which is our home. When we overlook the first miracle and do not feel at home within the larger universe it is impossible for us to feel at home within ourselves or with one another. The journey home, reconnecting with the first miracle of the universe around and within us, is a theme woven through this book.

In our long evolutionary ascent toward the third miracle of knowing ourselves, we have been pulling back from our connection with nature and the first miracle. I believe this has been a natural and purposeful process. The human family is on a collective journey to awaken and, in the initial phase, our evolutionary task was to separate ourselves from nature and to develop our sense of individuality and empowerment. We have now succeeded so well and become so empowered that we are disrupting the climate, depleting precious resources, spreading weapons of mass destruction, and overpopulating the Earth. We are hitting an evolutionary wall and being pushed by necessity—and pulled by opportunity—to make a great turn in our evolutionary journey. How do we find our way back to the living universe? How can we visualize ourselves at home in the universe?

To expand our appreciation of the universe, let's consider four observations from science that set the stage for a more systematic inquiry in the following chapter. These four insights always fill me with awe.

We Are Giants

When we gaze at the enormity of the universe, with its billions of swirling galaxies, it seems natural to conclude that we are very small. When we see a universe that extends trillions upon trillions of kilometers, it is reasonable to think we are insignificant in the cosmic scale of things. However, this commonsense view of ourselves is radically mistaken. We are not small creatures. In the overall scale of the universe, we are giants!

Imagine you have a ruler that measures from the largest scale of the known universe to the smallest. At the largest, we see hundreds of billions of galaxies, each containing billions of stars like our Sun.

At the smallest, we travel deep within the core of an atom to the world of quarks, and then farther, to the foundations of existence and what is called the "Planck distance."[3] If we were to place humans on that ruler, we would fall roughly in the middle zone.[4] Actually, we are a bit on the larger side, as shown in the accompanying illustration. The stunning insight from science is that *there is more smallness within us than there is bigness beyond us.*

In the cosmic scheme of things, we are actually enormous creatures who live in the middle range of the spectrum of cosmic existence. Thinking we are small represents a profound misperception. Just as we are stunned by the immensity of our universe, we should be equally amazed to learn of our own enormity. The universe reaches into unimaginably minute realms within us. We think of the realm of atoms as small, but there is a vast distance from the

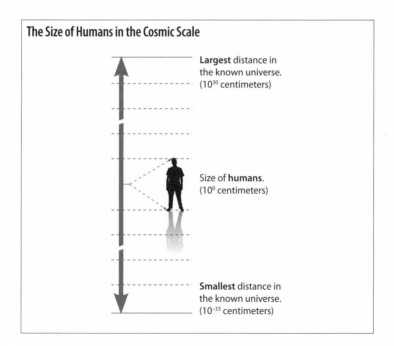

The Size of Humans in the Cosmic Scale

Largest distance in the known universe.
(10^{30} centimeters)

Size of **humans**.
(10^{0} centimeters)

Smallest distance in the known universe.
(10^{-33} centimeters)

size of atoms to the truly infinitesimal realms at the foundations of existence. It seems likely that a vast amount of harmonizing activity is occurring in the immensity that lies between the realm of atoms and the realm of the truly small.

Scientists consider our size as humans to be optimal for who we are. If we were significantly smaller, we would not have enough atoms to become the complex and intelligent creatures we are. If we were significantly larger, our nervous system would not operate fast enough to support rapid communication within our bodies. In the cosmic scale, we seem to be just the right size.[5]

Because we are giants, living in the mid-range of the cosmic scale of existence, we should not be surprised that we overlook much that happens on the smaller, more refined scale of the universe. As giants, it is easy for us to fail to notice the intense activity at the ultra-microscopic scale of the universe.

The Nearly Invisible Universe

Scientists long assumed that *visible* forms of matter and energy make up the universe. Recently, they were stunned to discover that an overwhelming preponderance of the universe is invisible. It is a scientific fact that we don't know what 96 percent of the universe really is. Scientists currently describe two major kinds of invisible energies in the universe. One is a contractive force called *dark matter* and the other is an expansive force called *dark energy*. They are called "dark" because they cannot be seen and measured by any direct means. Dark matter is thought to comprise roughly 23 percent of the universe.[6] The invisible mass of dark matter provides the gravitational field needed to keep whirling galaxies from flying apart as they spin. Dark energy is thought to comprise roughly 73 percent of the universe. This in-

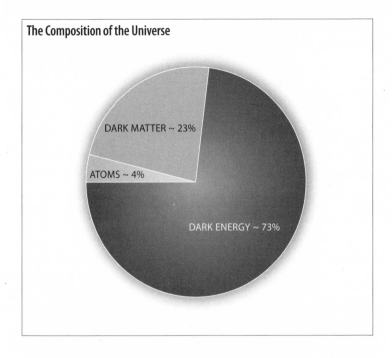

The Composition of the Universe

DARK MATTER ~ 23%

ATOMS ~ 4%

DARK ENERGY ~ 73%

visible energy permeates the universe and is causing it to inflate or expand from within at an increasing rate.[7] The remaining 4 percent comprises the entire visible universe of planets and stars.

If nearly all the universe is invisible, undetectable, and currently unknown, then we must expand our everyday understanding of the word "universe" accordingly. It is important to remember that, throughout this book, the word universe refers to much more than the familiar ingredients of matter and energy, because they constitute only a small fraction of a much larger reality.

If 96 percent of the known universe is invisible, then how much of ourselves is invisible and not detectable by material technologies? How far do we extend into the deep ecology of the invisible universe? Because we are an integral part of the universe, a large part of ourselves may well be connected with and operating in these invisible realms. The roots of our being reach deep.

Just Getting Underway

For centuries people looked at the world around us and assumed that it was a place of only three dimensions. Roughly a hundred years ago Einstein identified the fourth dimension—time—and the fabric of the universe came alive as a dynamic field. No longer is there such a thing as space, there is only *space-time.* A century later, cosmologists are further expanding the fabric of reality with string theories of eleven dimensions and more.[8] Indeed, many cosmologists now assume that the universe may have a countless number of additional dimensions. This is a stunning insight because each progressively larger dimension seems to offer dramatically new levels of freedom for life to express itself.

Although we may seldom think about dimensions, they are basic to the way reality works. Dimensions are far more than dry mathematical concepts—they are the invisible organizing substructures within which we exist. The miracle that anything exists at all depends upon dimensions to provide the organizing framework within which things can manifest in a coherent manner. Despite the pervasive dynamism of the universe, it holds together and presents itself as the stable, predictable world we see around us. Dimensions provide an invisible framework that keeps everything in its proper place and time (space-time), and bring coherence to the dynamism of the universe.

We can infer the presence of additional dimensions in the expansion of the universe. The popular image of the Big Bang is that of an explosion hurling matter out in all directions. This is misleading because it evokes the image of a pre-existing empty space into which matter is expanding. A more accurate image is that our universe is growing from the inside out, everywhere at once, with galactic islands using their gravitation to hold themselves together against the opening flow. It is the growing "roominess" of the universe, as the fabric of space-time expands, that produces the growing separation of galaxies. Because the fabric of space-time seems able to expand indefinitely, it points to the presence of even more spacious dimensions to accommodate this elasticity.

Assuming cosmologists are correct that there are an enormous number of additional dimensions, it is both important—and humbling—to recognize that we are not living in the 3,000th dimension or 300th dimension or even 30th dimension. We live in the third and fourth dimensions, at the very beginnings of existence, just a few steps above a black hole, or the collapse of reality into a single dimension. We live in a highly constricted reality, with an immensity of freedom and evolutionary opportunity beckoning us from more spacious dimensions. *We thought we were at the culmination of evolution, and we are now discovering that we are only at the beginning.* We are just moving out of the zone of collapse of matter into a black hole, and moving into the zone where life can encounter itself, know itself, and evolve itself. Vastly larger ecologies of life and learning likely exist in the spaciousness beyond our few contracted dimensions. Instead of the end of our journey, we seem to be at the very beginning of a voyage into infinity. It is a theme we will explore throughout this book.

Our Intuitive Connection with the Cosmos

Another remarkable discovery emerging from science is that we are not cut off from the rest of the universe. A core theme throughout this book is the idea that we each have an intuitive connection with the cosmos, even though it may be largely unrecognized and undeveloped. The respected author and researcher Dean Radin did an exhaustive analysis of psi research involving more than eight hundred studies and sixty investigators over nearly three decades.[9] After weighing the collective evidence from all these studies, he concluded that we do participate in a subtle field, or ecology, of consciousness where we can both "send" and "receive." These results are borne out in people's everyday experience. For example, surveys of the American adult population show that two-thirds say they have had an experience of extrasensory perception such as an accurate intuition about the well-being of someone who is far away.[10] In addition, about 40 percent report having had a "mystical" experience such as seeing the universe as alive and feeling a sense of great peace and safety within that aliveness.[11] In keeping with these findings, a recurring theme of this book is that consciousness is not confined within the brain but is an infusing presence throughout the universe that enables us, in cooperation with the brain, to connect meaningfully with the world beyond our physical body.

Bringing these four areas of insight together already begins to awaken the possibility of a new sense of ourselves, the universe, and the human journey. We thought we were small creatures living in a vast material universe. We believed that our capacity for thought put us at the peak of the evolutionary wave, but we have now been offered a very different view: *We are giants, living in a mostly invisible universe, who are just getting underway in our evolutionary journey, and can reach with our consciousness into the larger universe.* These freeing insights liberate us from thinking we are small and insignificant. Not incidentally, they also free us from the arrogance of thinking that we occupy the leading edge of evolution's wave.

Imagine Building a Universe

Imagine what would be required to create a cosmic system like ours. One of the most striking things about our universe is the extraordinary precision with which it is put together. The fine-tuning of dozens of key factors is essential because the most minute variation would have resulted in no universe at all. For example, had the rate of expansion after the Big Bang been even slightly faster, the universe would have evaporated—and no stars or planets would have formed. Alternately, had the rate of expansion been even slightly slower, the universe would have collapsed back upon itself long ago—and the Big Bang would have quickly become the Big Crunch! There are at least several dozen relationships in the universe that need to be precisely just as they are if life is to exist. From the strength of gravity to the charge of an electron—if any of these were different by even small amounts, life as we know it would not be possible. The extraordinary degree of fine-tuning in our universe indicates that a profound design-intelligence is at work (not to be equated with the theology of "intelligent design," which negates evolution).[12]

So what might be required to build and maintain, in good working condition, a universe like ours? Consider this: What if you are well known for your creativity and skill, and the Mother Universe says to you, "I really like your work. Would you like to build a cosmos? Think about it." Then the Mother Universe hands you nine design and construction requirements.[13] Consider these playfully as a way to stretch your imagination and prepare for the inquiry ahead.

- First, you must create a transparent field with an invisible structure called *geometry* that will keep everything in its proper place and time. Place the cosmos within that field and guarantee that this dimensional geometry will work flawlessly across trillions of miles for billions of years.

- Second, you cannot construct your universe from anything visible. You must build everything from transparent life energy.

- Third, instead of allowing the universe to emerge fully developed, you must engineer it so that it inflates from an area far smaller than a pinpoint and grows to contain a hundred billion galaxies, each with a hundred billion or more stars.

- Fourth, design *matter.* Take clouds of energy that are almost entirely empty space and have them flow around themselves trillions of times per second in order to present themselves as stable forms. Despite their completely dynamic nature, give these whirlwinds of energy the appearance and feel of solidity.

- Fifth, design *space.* Simple emptiness or the absence of matter won't do; instead, you must continually regenerate the transparency of space throughout the universe. The invisible fabric of space-time must be an opening process that continually unfolds to provide the transparent container within which matter, an equally dynamic process, can present itself.

- Sixth, design a cosmic information system that connects instantaneously across the entire universe. Anything that happens anywhere must be knowable everywhere, instantly.

- Seventh, design the potential for planetary-scale ecosystems to emerge that can grow billions of unique living organisms, such as plants and animals. Ensure that these organisms can feed off each other in a process sustainable for billions of years.

- Eighth, design the potential for self-reflective life forms that are able to self-evolve toward ever more complex and conscious entities.

- Ninth, design a process that enables the cosmos to be continuously regenerated in its entirety using the flow-through of stupendous amounts of energy. This flow of continuous creation must include the fabric of space-time, and all manifestations of matter, thought, feeling, and consciousness.

"If you can meet these nine construction requirements, you are ready to begin building a new universe," says the Mother Universe. Although these design requirements are adapted from my book *Awakening Earth*, written more than fifteen years ago, each time I return to them it awakens my appreciation of the power, wisdom, and subtlety embodied in our cosmos. Our universe is a supremely elegant masterwork of ongoing creation. Recognizing the magnificent feat of design engineering it represents, we look at ourselves and the world around us with new wonder and appreciation. Stretching our imagination in this way is useful preparation for our inquiry as we turn to look at our mysterious universe through the lens of science and ask: Is it reasonable to regard our universe as a living system? The pivotal nature of this question is summarized in the following table, which contrasts the perspectives of a dead or a living universe.

Contrasting a Dead and a Living Universe
Dead Universe

The universe is **non-living at the foundations.** The universe is a collection of mostly dead matter and empty space that is not fundamentally alive. At the foundations, the universe is a cold, barren, unfeeling, and spiritless place.

The cosmos has no apparent **purpose** so any meaning must come from what we construct for ourselves as social beings. When we die, "the lights go out." The **soul** is a superstition.

Consciousness is a product of biochemistry and is located in the brain. Consciousness is absent from the universe except in higher animals.

Because we live in a physical universe, the only potentials that we can cultivate are **materially based** (physical, emotional, and mental).

We are **bodily beings** who are seeking spiritual experiences. We may think about a spiritual realm but we are basically physical entities and the two are separate.

Creation ended with the big bang nearly 14 billion years ago. Since then, all that has happened is the progressive evolution of ancient matter into more complex forms.

Life mysteriously emerges from non-living matter as the forms become more complex. **From the lesser the greater emerges.** From non-life, emerges life.

The purpose in life is to achieve **material security and success** in a materially defined world.

A **dead universe tells no stories** so we can each make up our own stories and they will have equal validity because none of them will ultimately matter.

There are small islands of life in a **vast field of non-living space and dead matter.**

Materialism makes sense in a dead universe. We can protect ourselves from the surrounding deadness with material pleasures and demonstrate our significance with material projects and accumulations.

Because the world around us is dead, it is proper to **exploit that which is dead** on behalf of the most intensely living, which is ourselves.

A **dead universe is indifferent** to human concerns.

Living Universe

The universe is **alive at the foundations.** The universe is a unique kind of living entity that is sustained by the flow-through of phenomenal amounts of life energy. The cosmos is a single living creature that encompasses all living creatures within it and is filled with feeling and soulful learning at every level.

The cosmos is a **purposeful** learning system. When we die, the clear light remains but we may not recognize our subtle body if we have not made friends with the invisible qualities of our **soul** while we are alive.

Consciousness is a living field of life energy that permeates the cosmos and provides a reflective capacity for material forms at every scale throughout the universe.

Because we live in a living universe, our highest potential is to become *Homo sapiens sapiens* or beings who can recognize themselves as a **body of light, love, music, and knowing.**

We are **spiritual beings** having a bodily experience. Our bodies are biodegradable vehicles for acquiring soul-growing experiences. Every experience plants its feeling-knowing-resonance in our soul.

Creation is ongoing, a continuing process. The entirety of the cosmos is sustained, moment by moment, with the flow through of stupendous levels of life energy.

Life is the foundation of all existence. The life force that sustains the entire universe is fundamental and the aliveness manifest by beings such as ourselves is emergent. **From the greater, the lesser emerges.** From the greatness of the Mother Universe, we humble beings emerge.

The purpose in life is to **learn how to live in eternity.** It means developing our potentials for double wisdom as *Homo sapiens sapiens* and to make friends with ourselves so when we die we recognize our subtle Self.

A living universe is itself a **story of immense meaning and richness** as, within it, are the stories of a vast array and variety of life forms in their journey of awakening.

Islands of life are simply those places where the **field of consciousness has become intensified** and has gotten hold of itself.

Simplicity makes sense in a living universe. We are motivated to minimize the clutter, complexity, and stress of the material side of life and to engage more fully the juice and joy of aliveness itself.

Because all is alive and interconnected, **whatever I do to the world I ultimately do to myself.**

The universe is a garden for growing living systems. The cosmos is **compassionately non-interfering** in the unfolding of her offspring.

Chapter 2

The Science of a Living Universe

Everyone who is seriously involved in the pursuit of science
becomes convinced that a spirit is manifest in the laws
of the universe—a spirit vastly superior to that of men…
—ALBERT EINSTEIN[1]

This chapter applies the tools of science to explore the possibility that our universe, taken in its totality, is a living system. I am not seeking to *prove* that the universe is a living system; instead I will show that, by drawing insights from different areas of science, the available evidence *points strongly* in this direction and offers a compelling invitation for deeper engagement and inquiry.

In thinking about how the universe could be alive, we naturally turn to the living things already known. It is understandable that many of our theories on the nature of life are based on animals and plants; however, to confine our understanding of life to these familiar forms is to confuse the material expression of aliveness with the energy of aliveness itself. The form is not the aliveness, but its container. We need to broaden our inquiry into the meaning of life.

As mentioned earlier, it is the very tools of science that are challenging the traditional scientific assumption that the universe is non-living at its foundations. The powerful instruments of science are allowing us to peer down into the realm of atoms as well as out to the realm of stars. What we are discovering is astonishing; the deeper and further we look, the more complex, subtle, mysterious—and alive—the universe appears to be.

At the outset, it is important to recognize that the idea that we live in a non-living universe is a recent invention. The next chapter makes it clear that, throughout most of human history, we humans did not question whether the world around us was fundamentally alive. Only in the last few centuries that science has made a great separation between ourselves and the rest of the universe, assuming the universe to be mostly non-living matter with only a few islands of life such as ourselves.

In launching our inquiry, it is important to recognize that, within the scientific community, there is no widely accepted definition of life. To illustrate the difficulty scientists are encountering, there is no clear demarcation between the living and non-living realms. There is considerable debate, for example, over whether a virus is alive. By itself a virus is a non-living entity but when it finds a suitable host—such as a human being—it can rapidly replicate itself (think of the common cold) and evolve into new, more contagious forms. Because the ability to replicate and evolve is fundamental to life, a virus hovers in the gray zone between life and non-life.

Since we barely understand the mysterious property that we call life, it is not surprising that there is no broadly accepted definition. Is life an invisible energy or is it inseparable from the physical container of that energy? Many scientists focus on the container and say that living entities are carbon-based creatures that need water, get their energy either from the Sun or from a chemical source, and are able to reproduce themselves. Although this may be a fitting description of life on the Earth, it is such a narrow definition that it leaves little room for the possibility of alternative expressions.[2] While many scientists apply only a few criteria for describing a living system, I propose a demanding array of six criteria—a composite taken from a range of sources—for considering whether the universe is alive:

> Is the universe unified despite its great size?
> Is energy flowing throughout?
> Is it being continuously regenerated?
> Is there sentience or consciousness throughout?
> Is there freedom of choice?
> Is our universe able to reproduce itself?

This is a very challenging list of criteria for our universe to meet if we are to regard it as a living system. Let's consider them one at a time, drawing insights from respected sources in mainstream science and cosmology. These discussions are not fringe science; rather, they draw from well-established sources within the scientific community.

A Unified Universe

A living entity is a unified whole, not a random collection of disconnected parts. How could our universe, which appears to be mostly empty space with widely separated islands of matter, be unified? On the surface, our universe appears to be composed of separate components, from atoms to people to planets. How is it possible to regard these pieces as parts of a unified whole? Reflect for a moment on the scale of unity we are considering. Our home galaxy—the Milky Way—is a swirling, disk-shaped cloud containing a hundred billion stars. It is part of a local group of nineteen galaxies (each with a hundred billion stars of its own) that form part of a super-cluster of thousands of galaxies. Beyond this, astronomers estimate that there are perhaps a hundred billion galaxies in the observable universe (each, again, with a hundred billion stars). How could this vastness be regarded as an undivided whole?

One of the most stunning insights to emerge from modern science has been described as *non-locality.* The basic idea is simple: In the past, scientists have assumed that instant communication cannot take place between two distant points; instead, it takes time for a message to travel from one place to another, even at the speed of light. For example, it takes light about eight minutes to travel from the Sun to the Earth, which means that something could happen on the Sun and it would take eight minutes before we would know about it on Earth. Because other galaxies are millions of light-years away from us, they seem so remote as to be completely separate from our own existence. Yet scientific experiments show that, despite these vast distances that seem impossible to bridge, in reality everything in the universe is deeply interconnected.[3] Experiments have repeatedly demonstrated that subatomic particles are able to communicate *instantly* with one another, regardless of the distances that separate them.

The highly regarded physicist David Bohm explained this phenomenon by portraying the universe as a gigantic hologram that is regenerated at each moment. In Bohm's view, the entire cosmos is a dynamic projection from a deeper common ground that is holographic in nature. At every moment, every part of the universe contains information about the whole. Analogously, if you take a holographic picture of a person and then cut the plate in half, when each half is illuminated, it will contain the entire original image, although more faintly. If each of the halves is cut in half again, each of the pieces will contain a smaller but complete version of the original. The whole is in every part and every part is in the whole.

Nonlocality exists, not because of extremely fast messaging back and forth at the subatomic level, but because separation does not exist. Bohm said that ultimately we have to see the entire universe as "a single, undivided whole."[4] Instead of separating the universe into living things and non-living things, he viewed animate and inanimate matter as inseparably interwoven with the life force that is present throughout the universe. For Bohm, even a rock has its unique form of aliveness, because the life force is dynamically flowing through the fabric of the entire universe.[5] The eminent physicist John Wheeler expressed the unity of the universe in this way:

> Nothing is more important about the quantum principle than this, that it destroys the concept of the world as "sitting out there," with the observer safely separated from it.... To describe what has happened, one has to cross out that old word "observer" and put in its place the new word "participator." In some strange sense the universe is a participatory universe.[6]

In the earlier view of a universe composed of separate objects, we could regard ourselves as independent observers; however, in the new understanding of the universe, everything participates with everything else in co-creating reality, moment by moment. As stunning as it seems, non-locality means that we each participate in the totality of the universe. In the words of the physicist Sir James Jeans, we may think that we are "...individuals carrying on separate existences in space and time, while in the deeper reality beyond space and time we may all be members of one body."[7]

An Ocean of Background Energy

A second key property of living systems is that energy flows through them. What about our universe? Despite the vast reaches of seemingly empty space, is there evidence of energy flowing throughout the totality of the universe?

Nearly 14 billion years after the Big Bang, the expansion of the universe is not slowing down, as we would expect with a mechanical explosion; instead, it started picking up speed roughly 5 billion years ago. Trying to account for this expansion, scientists were shocked to discover that phenomenal amounts of energy are present throughout the universe and are pushing it apart. As mentioned in the opening chapter, it is thought that invisible or dark energy is causing our universe to expand at an increasing rate. Recall that scientists estimate dark energy comprises the majority of our cosmos—an estimated 73 percent of the universe.

Scientists also know that throughout the universe there exists a sea of background energy called *zero point energy*. It is called "zero point" because it is found at the lowest temperature that can exist in the universe—absolute zero. We cannot see zero point energy because it is everywhere and through everything and, as a result, it does not stand out. Although it is not yet clear how zero point energy is connected with dark energy, it is evident that stupendous amounts of background energy constantly flow through the universe. While we are just beginning to understand the nature of these remarkable energies, their existence is not disputed.

Whatever we call it, the background energy of the cosmos is shockingly large. Physicist David Bohm calculated that a single cubic inch of "empty" space contains far more than the energy equivalent of millions of atomic bombs![8] Empty space is a dynamically constructed transparency requiring immense amounts of energy to create and sustain. This underlying ocean of energy is the primary reality. This is not simply a theoretical abstraction; a number of scientists are working to invent technologies that can utilize this background energy.[9]

In recognizing the immensity of background energy in the cosmos, Bohm said that "...matter as we know it is...rather like a tiny ripple on a vast sea."[10] In a similar way, Sir James Jeans suggested that we think of the world that we see with our senses as the "outer surface of nature, like the surface of a deep flowing stream." He said that material objects have origins that go "deep down into the stream."[11]

A Continuously Regenerated Universe

Another key characteristic of living systems is continuous regeneration. To illustrate, consider how your body is being continuously renewed: The inner lining of your intestine is renewed roughly every five days, and the outer layer of your skin every two weeks. We receive a new liver approximately every two months, and the bones in our body are fully replaced about every seven to ten years. Clearly, an important attribute of any living creature is continuous regeneration. When we look for evidence of regeneration in the universe, what we discover is so stunning as to be virtually incomprehensible, even to the modern mind accustomed to great marvels. Simply stated, it appears that the entire universe is being continuously regenerated at an incredibly high rate of speed.

Until recently, the dominant cosmology in contemporary physics held that, since the Big Bang nearly 14 billion years ago, little more has happened than a rearranging of the cosmic furniture. Because traditional physicists thought of creation as a one-time miracle from "nothing," they regarded the current contents of the universe—such as trees, rocks, and people—as constituted from ancient, non-living matter. This "dead-universe" theory assumed creation occurred only once—billions of years ago, when a massive explosion spewed out lifeless material debris into equally lifeless space; "life" then somehow mysteriously emerged as non-living atoms inexplicably organized and grew themselves into ever more complex forms (molecules, cells, organisms).

In striking contrast, the living-universe theory views creation not as a one-time event but as an ongoing process. The entire universe is maintained moment-by-moment by an unbroken flow-through of energy. A regenerative perspective suggests why there is so much energy flowing through the universe—it is needed to continuously recreate the entire universe, including the fabric of space-time and matter-energy.[12]

If we go to the heart of an atom, for example, what we find is almost entirely empty space. If the central core or nucleus of an atom were expanded to the size of a golf ball, the electrons that circle the core would extend outwards a mile and a half. The electrons that circle the nucleus of the atom are moving so fast—several *trillion* times a second—that they manifest as a blurred cloud of motion. Beneath the solid surface of material objects, an extraordinary flow of activity is occurring. If you were to look at a yellow dress for just one second, the electrons in the retinas of your eyes would vibrate with more waves than all the waves that have beaten upon all the shores of all the Earth's oceans in the last 10 million years.[13] Physicist Max Born writes, "We have sought for firm ground and found none. The deeper we penetrate, the more restless becomes the universe; all is rushing about and vibrating in a wild dance."[14]

The deeper we look into the heart of matter, the less substantial it seems. Upon close inspection, matter dissolves into knots of energy and space-time whose dynamic stability gives the appearance of enduring solidity. It is amazing that this hurricane of flowing motion comes together to present itself as the ordinary world around us. As giants, it is easy for us to overlook the ongoing miracle that is taking place at a microscopic level.

If we go into the heart of space, what we find is dynamism, energy, and structure. Space is not a pre-existing emptiness waiting to be filled with matter; rather, like matter, it emerges anew at every moment. Space exists as actively as does matter. Both are infused with the all-sustaining life force. Empty space is a dynamically constructed transparency filled with immense levels of energy and motion. Einstein wrote, "We have now come to the conclusion that space is the primary thing and matter only secondary."[15] Erwin Schroedinger, father of quantum theory, stated it this way:

> What we observe as material bodies and forces are nothing but
> shapes and variations in the structure of space. Particles are just
> appearances...Subject and object are only one. The barrier
> between them cannot be said to have broken down...for this
> barrier does not exist.[16]

Physicist John Wheeler has used the following analogy to suggest how, upon closer inspection, the fabric of space-time comes alive with motion. He imagines an aviator flying several miles above the ocean who looks down and sees what appears to be a flat and uniform surface. When he flies lower, he begins to make out rolling waves moving across the surface. Diving still closer to the water, he sees smaller waves and crests forming on the swells. Looking even closer, he sees the surface of the water boiling with foam. In a similar way, the closer we look into the fabric of space-time, the more it appears as a complex symphony of waves and patterns; the smooth fabric of reality breaks down into "quantum foam" and our usual ideas of space and time disappear.

When we put the complete dynamism of matter together with the dynamism of space, it seems astonishing how stable and utterly dependable is the fabric of reality. We don't have to worry about "space-time storms" that might create rips and tears in the fabric of reality. It is extraordinary that complete dynamism at the microscopic scale manifests as a stable and unwavering reality at the human scale.

Given the dynamism of both matter and space, the universe is, in the words of David Bohm, "an undivided wholeness in flowing movement."[17] In this view, the entire cosmos is being regenerated at each instant in a single symphony of expression that unfolds from the most microscopic aspects of the subatomic realm to the vast reaches of billions of galactic systems. The cosmos taken altogether is the basic unit of continuous creation.

Scientists sound like poets as they attempt to describe our cosmos in its process of becoming. The mathematician Norbert Wiener expresses it this way: "We are not stuff that abides, but patterns that perpetuate themselves; whirlpools of water in an ever-flowing river."[18] Imagine water flowing over rocks in a stream. If we look at the flow over a particular rock, we can see a persisting pattern despite the continuous streaming of water. We, and the rest of the universe, are a persisting pattern that, as physicist Brian Swimme tells us, "emerges out of an all-nourishing abyss not only 14 billion years ago but in every moment."[19] All flows comprise one grand symphony in which we are all players, a single creative expression—a uni-verse.

Sentience at Every Level

The word *consciousness* derives from the root "con-scire" and means "that with which we know." Some level of consciousness is basic to life; therefore, if the universe is alive, we should expect to discover evidence of consciousness operating at every level of existence. This does not mean that we should expect to encounter *human* consciousness. We humans embody the third miracle, the capacity to see ourselves in the mirror of our own self-awareness. Our scientific name as a species is *Homo sapiens sapiens*. In other words, we are the species that is not only "sapient" or wise, but "sapient-sapient" or doubly knowing or doubly wise.[20] In contrast, the consciousness that we find at the foundations of the universe could be called "primary perception," or basic sentience. This refers to the capacity for knowing, but without the ability to reflect upon the knowing process itself.

When we look along the spectrum of existence, what do we find? At the most fundamental levels we find evidence of primary perception. The respected physicist Freeman Dyson wrote the following about consciousness at the quantum level: "Matter in quantum mechanics is not an inert substance but an active agent, constantly making choices between alternative possibilities.... It appears that mind, as manifested by the capacity to make choices, is to some extent inherent in every electron."[21] Again, this does not mean that an atom has the same consciousness as a human being, but rather that an atom has a reflective capacity appropriate to its form and function. In a similar vein, Max Planck, developer of quantum theory, said: "I regard consciousness as fundamental. I regard matter as derivative from consciousness. We cannot get behind consciousness."[22] In accepting the Nobel Prize, he said: "All matter originates and exists only by virtue of a force…. We must assume behind this force the existence of a conscious and intelligent mind. This mind is the matrix of all matter."

Looking one step above the level of the atom, we find a rudimentary consciousness present at the level of primitive molecules. Researchers have found that molecules consisting of no more than a few simple proteins have the capacity for primary perception that is the signature of living systems. As one of the researchers who made this discovery stated, "We were surprised that such simple proteins can act as if they had a mind of their own."[23]

Stepping up from molecules, we look at the smallest "living" entities, single-celled microbes that are found everywhere from inside our intestines to the scum on the surface of a pond. Scientists studying bacteria, amoebas, and yeast have discovered that they are intensely social creatures possessing unique forms of language. These single-cell creatures are not loners; instead, they are connected as a community and use chemicals to communicate with one another. This is amazing enough, but the truly remarkable finding is that the same chemical communication can have different meanings in different circumstances. Microbes are not unconscious machines but discerning organisms with a social intelligence previously considered possible only in the realm of intelligent animals such as primates.[24]

The behavior of slime mold is another clear illustration of sentience in the smallest organisms. Slime molds are primitive organisms that originated very early in Earth's history and are not classified as either a plant or an animal. For most of its life, slime mold exists as a single-cell organism, living in moist soil, feeding on decaying bark, leaves, and other matter on the forest floor. When the food supply runs out, something remarkable happens: between 10,000 and 50,000 individual cells come together to create a multicellular organism. Individual cells organize themselves, without the aid of an apparent leader, into a flower-like stalk supporting a ball of spores. This micro "super-organism" seems to have a will of its own and is able to move across a forest floor, responding to changes in light and temperature. Upon reaching a better feeding area, the multicellular entity releases its spores into the air, dispersing them into the more favorable feeding ground. New single cells grow from the spores and then go about their foraging as individuals.[25] Through its actions, slime mold demonstrates that, at the fundamental level of individual cells, some form of primary consciousness is able to communicate with the consciousness of other cells to co-create a larger entity. In turn, this larger entity is able to respond to the surrounding environment and to work for collective survival.

Another single-celled organism that is more conscious than we thought is the amoeba. Studying their microscopic feeding patterns in a Petri dish, scientists have discovered they demonstrate a rudimentary consciousness—they do not move about randomly; instead, they are able to remember the last turn they made as they go about looking for food.[26] Again we find a primary consciousness operating at the simplest levels of biological organization.

Turning to a higher level of complexity and the world of plants, scientists have found plants can communicate with one another using subtle odor molecules. Plants can send out chemical signals that repel insects; they can also attract insects that eat the pests that feed on their leaves. Not only can plants use chemical signals in their defense, they can also use them to warn other plants of danger, enabling their neighbors to jump-start their defenses.[27] Again, we find a rudimentary knowing or a discerning sentience.

When we turn to the world of animals, we find elements of human-like consciousness that indicate we are not unique, as we previously thought.[28] For example, self-recognition is not restricted to humans. Great apes, as well as elephants, dolphins, magpie birds, and pigeons, are able to recognize themselves in a mirror.[29] A capacity for empathy and feeling for another animal has been observed in primates, dolphins, whales, elephants, dogs, hippos, birds, and even some rodents. Elephants will remain by the body of a deceased member of their group for hours in an apparent gesture of respect, and this suggests the capacity for compassion. Tool making has been observed in crows, chimps, and bonobos (a species of great apes). Dolphins have also shown they can use tools; for example, they will sometimes use the spiny body of a dead scorpion fish to get a moray eel out of its hiding place. The ability to understand language has been observed in dolphins, bonobos, and parrots. Overall, there is a continuum of consciousness and an array of animals has demonstrated an active consciousness and a much richer cognitive life than previously suspected. Although we humans have an advanced capacity for reflective consciousness, we are not a unique and separate form of life; instead, we have simply progressed further along a spectrum of reflective consciousness.

Because we find evidence of primary perception or some form of consciousness operating at the level of atoms, molecules, single-cell organisms, plants, and animals, we should not be surprised that sentience is a basic property of the universe. It is when we move to the human realm that we find the most direct evidence that consciousness is not confined within the brain; it is, instead, a field property of the universe itself.

Although the topic is still controversial among more traditional scientists, the properties of consciousness have been a subject of intensive scientific research for more than forty years. Sometimes called psychic or "psi" research, this field explores a wide range of phenomena and human capacities that allow us to connect with the world beyond our physical bodies. In the previous chapter, I described the exhaustive inquiry of the consciousness researcher Dean Radin. Based upon decades of research, Radin concluded that consciousness is a capacity that includes both "receiving" and "sending" potentials. Let's consider each aspect of consciousness.

Evidence of the *receiving potentials* of consciousness comes from experiments on a type of psychic skill sometimes called "remote viewing." Remote viewing is the ability to gather meaningful information about a remote person or location by intuitive or non-physical means. In remote viewing, the receiver is not expected to acquire exact information, but intuitive impressions regarding, for example, the actions and location of a specific individual. Radin found that remote viewing has been "repeatedly observed by dozens of investigators using different methods."[30] He concluded that a capacity for conscious knowing "operates between minds and through space."

Evidence of the *sending potentials* of consciousness comes from experiments dealing with mind-matter interactions, such as the ability to influence the swing of a pendulum clock. Radin concluded that "After sixty years of experiments...researchers have produced persuasive, consistent, replicated evidence that mental intention is associated with the behavior of physical systems."[31]

I would be reluctant to write so specifically about consciousness as a permeating property of the universe had I not had the opportunity to learn about this first hand in a scientific laboratory. The opportunity to explore our intuitive connections with the cosmos arose unexpectedly. As mentioned in the introduction, in the early 1970s I was working as a senior social scientist at the think tank SRI International doing studies of the long-range future. At that time

I was invited to participate in the psychic research experiments that were launched on behalf of NASA by two senior physicists, Harold Puthoff and Russell Targ.[32] One experiment grew into several and over the next three years I would often spend several days each week in their engineering laboratory where, for several hours at a time, I was engaged in both formal and informal experiments. Results from the formal, rigorously controlled experiments have been reported in some of the most prestigious science and engineering journals in the world.[33] After the success of the early years, the psi research became a secret project of the CIA and I chose to drop out because of ethical considerations—I did not want to contribute to an exploration of the potential for psychic warfare. Many years later, I learned that the CIA continued to fund this research for two more decades.[34]

As mentioned earlier, during the time I was intensely involved with the psychic research, I was also deeply involved with meditation, primarily Buddhist approaches to mindfulness and concentration. With powerful synergy, the combination of intense meditation and feedback from impartial scientific experiments gave me useful tools for learning about the ecology of consciousness.

To illustrate our capacity for intuitive knowing, I'd like to return to remote viewing and briefly describe a series of controlled experiments in which I was involved. In practical terms, the procedure for testing "seeing at a distance" was of stark simplicity. I was locked in a bare room with a pad of paper, a pencil, and a tape recorder and then asked, after waiting half an hour for the travel time of my colleague, to describe the area surrounding the location of the outbound experimenter. The target person was someone I knew well, so I could intuitively connect with them. After my door was locked, the destination of the outbound person was selected by another scientist (not otherwise involved in the experiment) by drawing an envelope at random from a locked safe that contained more than a hundred possible locations. My task was to describe in words and drawings the location of the distant person. Was he on a boat in the bay? In a car on the freeway? In a grove of redwood trees? In a movie theater? In the room next door? My only instructions were, "Take a deep breath, close your eyes, and tell us what you see." Although impressions were subtle and fleeting, I gradually learned that we all have an intuitive ability to "see" at a distance. Through our intuition, each of us can acquire useful impressions, images, and insights about a distant person or place. In my experience and that of other subjects, the descriptions were sufficiently accurate to be matched with the actual locations to a statistically significant degree.[35]

Instead of an unusual capacity accessible to only a special few, I think remote viewing—using our intuitive capacities to connect with the world at a distance—is a *universally accessible capacity*. Our perceptions may be momentary, but they can still contain accurate and useful information. With practice, we can extend our consciousness, "tune in" to the larger world, and receive impressions that, while fleeting and sketchy, still have a measure of accuracy. Many people already recognize our inborn capacity for intuitive knowing. As mentioned in Chapter 1, national surveys in the United States indicate that two-thirds or more of the adult population report having some kind of extrasensory or intuitive experience.

I was also involved with another set of psychic experiments that explored the "sending" aspects of consciousness, or the potential to interact with matter via our intuitive faculties, which is sometimes called *psychokinesis*. To explore the sending, or expressive, aspect of consciousness, SRI researchers assembled instruments from one of the finest engineering and research laboratories in the world. A range of experimental apparatus was set up for me to interact with, and learn from, over a period of several years. In one experiment, I was able to move a clock pendulum, sitting at rest, while a laser beam registered and recorded the movement on a strip-chart recorder. In a second experiment, I engaged a "frozen" electrical field by interacting with a sensor placed inside a canister of extremely cold, liquid helium while the interactions were registered on a strip-chart recorder, sometimes far outside the "noise level" or random variation of the system. In a third experiment, I "pressed" on a highly sensitive scale that was locked in another room and connected to a strip-chart recorder that registered any motion.

Unlike the highly controlled remote viewing experiments, the psychokinesis experiments were largely exploratory and informal. With the more relaxed laboratory conditions, I would spend several hours at a time exploring my intuitive connection with the experimental apparatus. My primary motivation was to understand how the cosmos worked—and the feedback was powerful and convincing. As I learned through trial and error over a period of nearly three years, I received striking evidence that we all participate in a subtle though powerful ecology of consciousness.

I took away a number of important insights from these diverse experiments in what might be called "cosmic feedback training." First, we *all* have an intuitive faculty and literal connection with the universe. An empathic connection with the cosmos is not restricted to a gifted few, it is an ordinary part of the functioning of the universe and is accessible to everyone.

Second, participating in these experiments demonstrated to me that our being does not stop at the edge of our skin but extends into and is inseparable from the universe. We are *all* connected with the deep ecology of the universe and each of us has the ability to extend our consciousness far beyond the range of our physical senses. I am reminded of the wisdom of George Washington Carver, a great educator and botanical researcher, who said that "If you love it enough, anything will talk with you."

Third, our intuitive connection with the cosmos is easy to overlook. Before I became involved in these experiments, I didn't pay much attention to the small, intuitive twinges and feelings that would arise and then pass away. They seemed so subtle that I assumed they were simply part of my bodily experience. Only gradually did I come to appreciate the extent to which I was experiencing my participation in a larger field of aliveness.

Fourth, I learned that psi functioning is not about achieving dominance over something (mind *over* matter) but rather learning to participate with something in a dance of mutual exchange and transformation. This is a two-way process in which both parties are changed by the interaction.

Fifth, at the same time these experiments were convincing me that consciousness is a field property of the universe, they also made me much more skeptical about the need for channeling, crystals, pendulums, pyramids, and other intermediaries to access our intuition. Validating consciousness as a basic property of the universe does not automatically validate all claims of paranormal phenomena. It is important to bring a critical and discerning science to this inquiry. We are just beginning to use the tools of science to cut away the superstition and find what is real and what is not. Our universe is a place of miracles, but it is not a place of magic. It is a miracle that anything exists at all. However, once the miracle of our universe exists, we find lawful dynamics at work throughout.

Sixth, scientific evidence of the existence of psychic functioning has been mounting for decades and is now so overwhelming that the burden of proof has shifted to those who would seek to dismiss its existence.[36] It is time to move beyond the narrow, brain-based view of consciousness because it no longer explains important scientific evidence and it severely limits our thinking about the scope and depth of our connection with the universe.

Seventh, as interesting as psychic or intuitive functioning may be, the much more important insight is what it says about the nature of the universe—that it is connected with itself through the tissue of consciousness in non-local ways that transcend relativistic differences.

To summarize, evidence is accumulating across many levels, from the atomic to the human, that a field of consciousness pervades the universe and is mobilized by different living systems in ways that support and sustain their functioning. While the idea of an underlying ecology of consciousness and aliveness is quite remarkable, it seems no more extraordinary than the widely accepted view among scientists that the universe emerged nearly 14 billion years ago as a "vacuum fluctuation," where nothing pushed on nothing to create everything.[37]

Freedom at the Foundations

Another attribute of living systems is their freedom to make choices. Without some measure of freedom of choice, we exist as meaningless machines. Is our universe a mechanical system without authentic freedom at its foundations? Or is it a living system that has the freedom to grow and develop in innovative ways?

The old Newtonian paradigm envisioned a deterministic universe where, once the laws governing things were understood, everything could be predicted. In striking contrast, findings from quantum physics tell us that uncertainty is built into the fabric of the universe. At the quantum level, where our universe comes into existence, the certainty that we find at the larger scales breaks down and, instead, we find only probabilities. At the foundation of the universe is the quantum foam seething with titanic energies, and this is where we enter a realm of likelihood, of possibilities and estimated outcomes. Freedom and uncertainty are basic to the quantum level, where the universe continuously recreates itself and provides us with an opportunity to exercise our freedom to do the same.

Freedom permeates our lives. We are playing jazz together. The world is a collective improvisation, and we have the creative freedom to transcend the habits of nature. While uncertainty and freedom are fundamental to our universe, freedom is not without limits. Everything that exists contributes to the overall cosmic web at each moment, whether it is conscious of its participation or not. In turn, it is the interrelation of all parts of the universe that determines the condition of the whole. We, therefore, have great freedom to act, but only within the limits established by the larger web of life.

Able to Reproduce Itself

An essential capacity for any living system is the ability to reproduce itself. How could our universe produce offspring universes? A startling insight from the frontiers of physics suggests the answer: Our universe may be able to reproduce itself through the functioning of black holes. Astrophysicist John Gribbin explains that the bursting out of our universe in the Big Bang is the time-reversed mirror image of the collapse of a massive object into a black hole. Many of the black holes that form in our universe, he reasons, may represent wormholes that lead to new universes: "Instead of a black hole representing a one-way journey to nowhere, many researchers now believe that it is a one-way journey to somewhere—to a new expanding universe in its own set of dimensions."[38] Gribbin's dramatic conclusion is that our own universe may have been birthed this way out of a black hole in another universe. He explains:

> If one universe exists, then it seems there must be many—very many, perhaps even an infinite number of universes. Our universe has to be seen as just one component of a vast array of universes, a self-reproducing system connected only by the "tunnels" through space-time (perhaps better regarded as cosmic umbilical cords) that join a "baby" universe to its "parent."[39]

The insight that there could be many universes evolving through time is not recent. Philosopher David Hume noted in 1779 that many prior universes "might have been botched and bungled throughout an eternity [before our universe]."[40] A growing number of cosmologists are now suggesting a universe evolves like other living systems—by passing along favorable characteristics to their offspring: "Universes that are 'successful' are the ones that leave the most offspring."[41] Many cosmologists now consider our universe to be one of many universes, all existing within a vastly larger universe that is sometimes called the "Meta-Universe" or "Master Universe" or "Multiverse."[42] I give this a friendlier name and call the generative source and sustainer of all the island universes the "Mother Universe."

An Integrative View from Science

When we bring together these findings from science, an extraordinary picture begins to emerge: Our universe is a profoundly *unified* system in which the interrelations of all the parts determine at every moment the condition of the system as a whole. Our universe is permeated and sustained by an unimaginably immense amount of flowing *energy;* it is being *continuously regenerated* in its entirety while making use of a knowing capacity or *consciousness* throughout. The universe appears to have *freedom* as a fundamental property of the quantum foundations as well as the ability to *reproduce* itself by using black holes as wormholes for creating a new cosmic system.

Combining these key characteristics, we can now see the whole-systems logic of the definition given in the introduction: *A "living universe" is a unified and completely interdependent system that is continuously regenerated by the flow-through of phenomenal amounts of life energy whose essential nature includes consciousness or a self-reflective capacity that enables systems at every scale of existence to exercise some freedom of choice.* The universe also has other characteristics of living systems such as the ability to reproduce itself via black holes that provide the seed instructions for growing new cosmic systems.

Because the universe appears to meet each of the key criteria for "aliveness," current scientific evidence points toward the conclusion that the universe is a living system. While these combined properties do not prove the universe is a living system, they point clearly in that direction. Because our universe embodies core properties that are common to living systems, from a scientific perspective, it seems compelling to explore the universe as a unique kind of living system.

We have explored a scientific definition of the universe as a living system. Now we turn to consider how that connects with us as human beings. How is our understanding of who we are and the journey we are on transformed by living in a living universe?

Part Two

Who Are We?

Chapter 3

Spirituality as Intimacy with a Living Universe

*At bottom, the whole concern of religion is
with the manner of our acceptance of the universe.*
—WILLIAM JAMES

Who we are depends directly upon *where* we are. Are we an inseparable part of a greater aliveness? Or are we a small speck of life that is surrounded by a vast sea of deadness? How do the world's wisdom traditions view the universe and our relationship to it? Do they see this world as a place of deadness to leave behind and move beyond? Or, do the wisdom traditions see the universe as a miracle of stunning aliveness? When people around the world and across the centuries offer their in-depth accounts of the nature of existence, what descriptions of the universe emerge? When sages and saints across cultures and history have come to a place of profound centeredness and quiet, what has become self-evident to them regarding the nature of the universe and our place within it?

For more than three decades, I have been exploring how the world's wisdom traditions view the universe. At the outset, I did not know what I would discover. Although views of the world's spiritual traditions are fairly well known when it comes to themes such as love and compassion, it was not clear to me how they regarded the universe. Might wisdom traditions regard the universe as something "out there" and largely separate from the spiritual quest "in here"? Or, is our relationship with the universe seen as integral to our spiritual awakening and development?

To show how wisdom traditions view the universe, I have drawn from a range of sources: Christian, Islamic, Hindu, Buddhist, Taoist, Confucian, Indigenous, and more. I realize there are deep differences, both within these traditions and between them. The clash of religions is a powerful and unsettling reality in today's world. Nonetheless, if we allow for their many differences, and look at the way each tradition regards the universe, I think the similarities we discover are striking and of immense importance in revealing a common understanding shared by all wisdom traditions. Common themes emerge as different spiritual traditions describe their in-depth understanding of our common home, the universe. Often it is the more mystical tradition within a spiritual family that explores these depths most fully. Given differences of history, culture, and geography, it is not surprising that each of the world's spiritual traditions would have a different way of describing the universe. It is important to receive each tradition on its own terms and allow it to speak for itself and inform us with its unique insights.

We will explore views of the universe through the lens of a half-dozen wisdom traditions that comprise a majority of the world's population. Although all belief systems deserve consideration, these few embrace the overwhelming majority of the human family and provide us with a strong foundation for this overview. As a cautionary note, I recognize that some people may not give much attention to how their spiritual tradition regards the universe. Nor do people necessarily hold a view of the universe consistent with their particular faith. With care to not overstate humanity's beliefs about the universe, let's explore how the world's spiritual traditions view the universe and humanity's relationship to it.

Judeo-Christian Views

Christianity, Judaism, and Islam have common roots in the idea of a single God. Despite their differences, all three religions trace their lineage back to the Hebrew patriarch Abraham whose life is described in the Jewish Bible known to Christians as the Old Testament (in the book of Genesis). From Abraham we find the core belief in a single, all-knowing, all-powerful, and transcendent God who created the universe as "good" and continues to be involved in its existence.

It is important to acknowledge that, for many, the word *God* tends to evoke the image of a remote masculine authority figure who is separate from this world. However, another view runs through both Judiasm and Christianity and uses the word *God* to evoke the image of a powerful, boundless spiritual presence that infuses, sustains, and transcends the universe. It is this latter meaning of God that is the focus of this inquiry.

The Judaic view of the origin of the universe is described in the first sentence of the first book of the Bible. In Genesis 1:1, we read that G–d (a deity beyond words and whose name cannot be written) created this universe out of nothing. "In the beginning God created the heavens and the Earth."[1] The word *created* comes from the translation of the Hebrew word "bara" and means to bring forth out of nothing.[2]

In Exodus (3:14), God reveals his name as "I AM THAT I AM."
God is without limits or boundaries. God simply is. Also in the Jewish Bible (and Old Testament), we find this powerful description of a
spiritual presence creating and sustaining the universe:

> The heavens declare the glory of God, the skies proclaim the
> work of his hands...
>
> —PSALMS 19:1[3]

Another translation of this Psalm is written differently. Instead of
saying "the heavens *declare* the glory..." it says, "the heavens *are
telling* of the glory..." The phrase "are telling" suggests the heavens
are being presented to beholders as an active, ongoing process.[4] The
heavens are proclaiming the magnificence of their creator as a continuing dynamic.

Here is another Psalm that describes an infusing spiritual presence throughout the universe:

> Where can I go from your Spirit? Where can I flee from your
> presence? If I go up to the heavens, you are there; if I make my
> bed in the depths, you are there. If I rise on the wings of the
> dawn, if I settle on the far side of the sea, even there your hand
> will guide me, your right hand will hold me fast.
>
> —PSALMS 139:7–10[5]

Overall, Judaism views the universe as a divine creation and humans
as having a direct relationship with its creative unfolding. Christianity has drawn from these roots and, with roughly one-third of humanity as adherents at the turn of the twenty-first century, it is the
world's largest religion. To explore the connection between Christianity and the cosmos, it is important to begin by acknowledging the

theological complexity of Christianity, with its many voices, institutions, and shifting emphases over time.

As theologians reexamine Christian history, one of the themes being explored is the idea that God not only creates and sustains the universe, but that the universe actually participates in the *being* of God. Here are quotes from the Bible that suggest a view of "God" as a divine spiritual presence that creates the universe and continues to be present within it.

> In him we live, and move, and have our being.... We are his offspring.
>
> —ACTS 17:28

> Through him all things came to be, not one thing had its being but through him.
>
> —JOHN 1:3

Christianity sees the universe as a divine creation permeated by a spiritual presence that celebrates the glory of its creator. In the New Testament book of Hebrews 11:3 we read, "...the universe was formed at God's command, so that what is seen was not made out of what was visible."[6] What we see around us is not made of anything visible. Recalling the preceding chapter, this is congruent with modern cosmology describing the birth of the universe from nothing as a "vacuum fluctuation."

The idea of a living universe is found explicitly and powerfully in the Eastern Orthodox Churches that comprise the world's third-largest Christian community after Catholicism and Protestantism. Eastern Orthodox Christianity holds the view that God's energies are vital for anything to exist at all and, for things to continue to exist, God's active involvement is essential. God's active presence is required to sustain the universe at every scale, from the most minute to the most grand. Because everything is upheld equally and without favor, this means that the entirety of creation is equally valued and sacred. God's energies sustain even those beings who reject the idea of God. God will not abandon creation, as nothing is viewed as existing separately from God. Beings may not be conscious of their communion with God, but God is ever conscious of us.

The idea that God is not separate from this world but is present within it is found in other Christian sources. Perhaps the most exciting was the discovery in 1945 of a collection of fifty-two religious and philosophical texts, not far from the village of Nag Hammadi in Upper Egypt. Experts estimate that they had been hidden in an earthenware jar for roughly 1,600 years. This was an enormously important discovery as it includes texts that were thought to have been destroyed during the early Christian struggles to define orthodox Christianity. The Nag Hammadi texts did not fit the accepted views of the times, so they were apparently sealed in a jar and hidden in a cave until they could be safely brought back to the public.

The most famous of these texts, The Gospel of Thomas, opens with these stunning words: "These are the secret sayings that the living Jesus spoke," and continues, "Whoever discovers the interpretation of these sayings will not experience death." What does Jesus have to say in this gospel that shifts our view of death from an ending to a transformation? In the Gospel of Thomas, when Jesus was asked, "When will the new world come?" He replied, "What you look forward to has already come but you do not recognize it." Elsewhere Jesus says, "...the Kingdom of the Father is spread out upon the earth, and people do not see it." Jesus is clearly saying that what we are looking for—the divine presence—is around us and within us. Jesus says, "The kingdom is inside of you, and it is outside of you. When you know yourselves, then you will become known, and you will realize that you are the children of the living Father. But if you do not know yourselves, then you live in poverty, and you are the poverty."

Moving forward in history, in 1215 the Catholic Church put forth the idea of *creatio ex nihilo* as official church doctrine, declaring God to be "Creator of all things, visible and invisible...out of nothing." In the 1300s, the great Christian mystic and theologian, Meister Eckhart, expanded on this theme and wrote "God is creating the entire universe, fully and totally, in this present now. Everything God created...God creates now all at once."[7] No declaration could be more specific or explicit concerning our universe as a continuously renewing system.

A number of Christian theologians now hold the view that God created our vast cosmos from nothing (*ex nihilo)* and that God upholds the universe through time (*creatio continua).*[8] Continuous creation is the pouring forth of the universe in a continual flow, without ceasing, over billions of years.[9] The world around us is seen as an ever-emerging miracle of divine generosity, continually emerging from an invisible source. Creation is always new, always fresh, and always alive. The Catholic Church now teaches that creation is always journeying towards its ultimate perfection. Evolution, therefore, poses no obstacle to genuine faith, as Pope John Paul II said in 1985. Instead, he said, "Evolution presupposes creation...creation is an ever-lasting process—a *creatio continua.*"

Although there are many differences within the Christian tradition, there exists a strong thread that sees our universe as a sacred body upheld by a divine presence in a process of continuous creation.[10]

Islamic Views

Islam has its roots in the same tradition of a single God as Christianity and Judaism. The word *Islam* means submission in Arabic, and Islam asks its followers to surrender their lives to Allah or God. This dynamic faith emerged in the seventh century with the prophet Muhammad (570–632), a native of Mecca in Arabia. Within a century of his death, an Islamic state stretched from the Atlantic Ocean to central Asia. Today, with nearly one and a half billion followers, Islam is the second-largest religion in the world.

Muslims believe Muhammad to be the final prophet of God. Over a period of twenty-three years, Muhammad received a series of revelations that were recorded by his followers. These revelations later became the Koran (Qur'an), the central religious text of Islam, believed by Muslims to be the word of God or Allah as revealed to Muhammad. Here the relationship of God to the universe is very explicit: "God is the Creator of everything; is the One, the Omnipotent." Not only is God the source and originator of everything but also its sustainer: "God keeps a firm hold on the heavens and earth, preventing them from vanishing away. And if they vanished no one could then keep hold of them. Certainly He is Most Forbearing, Ever-Forgiving." (Koran 35:41).

The Islamic view of God sustaining the universe is called *occasionalism* and describes the universe as being continuously reborn in a series of unique occasions or events.[11] Al-Ghazali, who lived in the eleventh century, was a celebrated theologian and great synthesizer of Muslim thought. He advanced the Islamic view that our universe is not an ancient, static structure; instead, it is born anew at each moment—created out of nothing in a series of events by the will of Allah.[12] Nothing continues to exist unless God constantly re-creates it. The book that you are holding now will be, in a moment, a new "occasion" of the book that went before it. Nothing endures in time; rather, everything comes into existence freshly in each moment, only to disappear and be replaced an instant later by another fresh expression or occasion.

Another major Islamic teacher is Ibn Arabi, who lived in the thirteenth century. Arabi wrote more than 300 works and had a powerful influence on Islamic spirituality. Even during his lifetime, he was considered one of the great spiritual teachers within Sufism, the esoteric tradition within Islam that focuses on direct experience of the divine. The central doctrine of Sufism is that all phenomena are manifestations of a single reality and arise out of a deep unity. According to Arabi, we do not notice the world is coming into existence and then passing away at every moment because, when one expression of existence passes away, it is immediately replaced by another nearly like it. He says that in thinking the world endures from past to present to future, we overlook the reality that, at every moment, the world presents a new creation of itself.

Rumi is an internationally famous, thirteenth-century Persian poet and Sufi.[13] His works have been translated into many languages, and his influence transcends ethnic and spiritual borders. Rumi wrote clearly about the continuous arising of existence: "You have a death and a return in every moment.... Every moment the world is renewed but we, in seeing its continuity of appearance, are unaware of its being renewed." He also said that life is like a stream: "it arrives new and fresh at every moment while it appears constant in its material form."

Mahmud Shabistari is another celebrated Persian poet. He wrote the following in 1317 c.e.:

The world is this whole, and in every twinkling of an eye,
it becomes non-existent and endures not two moments.

There over again another world is produced,

every moment a new heaven and a new earth.

Things remain not in two moments,

the same moment they perish, they are born again.

Finally, A. H. Almaas, a modern-day teacher with roots in the Sufi tradition, has written powerfully about all of existence continually coming into being: "The universe is never old; it is always new, for it includes both animate and inanimate objects, the Earth and the sky, the planets, the Sun and the stars, the galaxies and the space that contains them; it also includes all the thoughts, images, memories, feelings, sensations, and all phenomena at all levels of being."[14] All of this, says Almaas—the one totality that continuously comes into being—is something that we can experience directly.

Hindu Views

Hinduism dates back at least thirty-five hundred years and is the oldest and perhaps most complex of the world's living religions. It has no identified founder, but is known by its Vedas, or scriptures. Hinduism is the third-largest religion in the world with roughly 14 percent of the world's population, the majority of whom live in India. Although the term *Hinduism* encompasses many diverse sects and philosophies, all Hindus believe in a supreme cosmic spirit called *Brahman*. Brahman is the sustaining life force that is ultimately beyond description and the reach of human language. Brahman is the foundation of existence, and the source of all things as all things participate in the being of Brahman. By practicing different forms of meditation, Hindus believe that we can directly experience our sacred nature as Brahman. Atman, our individual essence or soulful nature, *is* Brahman—the sustaining cosmic spirit whose nature is often described as infinite being, infinite consciousness, and infinite bliss.

At the heart of the Hindu view of reality is the belief that our universe is continuously upheld by a divine life force. Huston Smith, scholar of the world's religions, writes, "All Hindu religious thought denies that the world of nature stands on its own feet. It is grounded in God; if he were removed it would collapse into nothingness."[15] In the words of a revered Hindu teacher, Sri Nisargadatta Majaraj, "The entire universe contributes incessantly to your existence. Hence the entire universe is your body."[16]

We are continually created from Brahman, and therefore at the most fundamental level, all things are one, unified, whole. The Bhagavad-Gita, written roughly 2,500 years ago, is one of the main holy texts of India. There, Brahman is described as the "king of all knowledge." The Gita states: "This entire universe is pervaded by Me, the unmanifest Brahman. All beings depend on Me. I do not depend on them." "I am the origin or seed of all beings. There is nothing, animate or inanimate, that can exist without Me.... the creator exists in the creation by pervading everything... He is inside as well as outside of all beings, animate and inanimate. He is incomprehensible because of His subtlety. He is very near as well as far away."

Turning to even older sources of wisdom in the Hindu tradition, the texts of the Upanishads, we find this declaration:

Out of himself he brought forth the cosmos
And entered into everything in it.
There is nothing that does not come from him.
Of everything he is the inmost Self.
He is the truth; he is the Self supreme.
You are that... you are that.
— CHANDOGYA UPANISHAD

Hindu mythology portrays the cosmos being born anew at each moment through the cosmic dance of Shiva. "Nature and all its creatures are the effects of his eternal dance."[17] All expressions and aspects of the living world are but momentary flashes from the limbs of the Lord of the dance.[18] In the Hindu view of the universe, there is nothing permanent; rather, the cosmos is seen as one body being continuously danced into creation by the divine life force.

For a more contemporary Hindu perspective, the writing of the revered sage and philosopher Sri Aurobindo is insightful. He wrote: "...there is but one Force in the world, a single unique current which passes through us and all things...it is this force which links up everything, animates everything; this is the fundamental substance of the Universe."[19] Finally, when Mahatma Gandhi, the great spiritual and political leader of India, was asked what he considered to be the essence of Hinduism, he quoted the first verse of the Isha Upanishad, which begins with these lines:

Filled with Brahman are the things we see,
Filled with Brahman are the things we see not,
From out of Brahman floweth all that is:
From Brahman all—yet is he still the same.[20]

Again and again, in Hinduism, we find the theme of a life force continuously regenerating the universe in a dance of cosmic-scale creation. Heinrich Zimmer, the respected scholar of Indian art and civilization, summarizes Hindu cosmology by saying: "There is nothing static, nothing abiding, but only the flow of a relentless process, with everything originating, growing, decaying, vanishing."[21]

Buddhist Views

Buddhism is a family of wisdom traditions and its followers comprise about 6 percent of the world's population. These traditions have their origins in the historical person of Siddhartha Gautama, who was born in the foothills of the Himalayas in India in the sixth century B.C.E. Siddhartha was an Indian prince who eventually renounced his power and wealth to meditate on the nature of reality. After his "enlightening experience" other monks saw his newly discovered radiance and knowing, and asked him, "Are you a God?" He replied no. They then asked if he were an angel? Again he answered no. "Then what are you?" they asked. He replied simply: "I am awake."[22] He became known as the Buddha, which means "the one who is awake." After his awakening, he taught for the remaining forty-five years of his life, traveling through northeastern India, teaching and mentoring a diverse community of people. Primarily, he taught that, through meditation and spiritual inquiry, anyone could awaken from the sleep of ignorance and directly realize the nature of the universe and their own nature.

What was the core realization that the Buddha awakened to? At the foundation of the Buddha's teachings is his description of the simultaneous arising of all things in the universe. Variously translated as "interdependent co-arising" and "interdependent co-origination," the Buddha said this insight was at the heart of his awakening. According to the Buddha, to discern the moment-to-moment, interdependent co-arising of all things in the universe is to awaken to a reality that is subtle, sublime, hard to perceive, and not accessible through logic alone. Because the co-arising of all things in the universe is a process that completely includes us, we cannot stand back to observe it; instead, to know this reality we must relax completely into ourselves and become transparent to more subtle levels of our own experience. When we consciously experience ourselves in this way, we find nothing permanent; instead we find complete dynamism and flow, including the direct experience of ourselves.

From the perspective of Tibetan Buddhism, the Dalai Lama has written, "At the heart of Buddhist cosmology is not only the idea that there are multiple world systems...but also the idea that they are in a constant state of coming into being and passing away."[23] The Tibetan teacher, scholar, and artist Lama Govinda writes, "The world is in a continuous state of creation, of becoming, and therefore in a continuous state of destruction of all that has been created."[24] He also writes, "This apparently solid and substantial world [is]...a whirling nebulous mass of insubstantial, eternally rotating elements of continually arising and disintegrating forms."[25] Namkhai Norbu, another esteemed teacher in the Tibetan Buddhist tradition, states, "All phenomena...no matter how solid they may seem, are in fact essentially void, impermanent, only temporarily existing."[26]

Because the world around us is being continuously regenerated—arising freshly in its totality at each moment so absolutely nothing endures—it makes sense that the Buddha would describe existence as a "flash of lightning in a summer cloud," a "flickering lamp," an "apparition," and a "phantom." The world flashes into existence as a unified whole at one moment—presenting itself in all its vividness—only to disappear completely and be replaced an instant later with a new representation of itself. In learning the skills of meditation, the Buddha said we can become centered in the flow of natural time and experience directly the co-arising of the cosmos.

Turning from the Buddhism of Tibet to that practiced in Japan, we again find this insight of the moment-to-moment arising of the universe. The respected Zen scholar and teacher, D. T. Suzuki, has written, "My solemn proclamation is that a new universe is created every moment."[27] Elsewhere he writes, "All things come out of an unknown abyss of mystery, and through every one of them we can have a peep into the abyss."[28] Also from the Zen tradition we have this unequivocal statement from Alan Watts: "The beginning of the universe is now, for all things are at this moment being created, and the end of the universe is now, for all things are at this moment passing away."[29] Others in the Zen tradition describe the continuous arising of the universe. Robert Linssen describes the world seen through the eyes of a skilled meditator: "A tree, a stone, an animal cease to be seen as solid and durable bodies...in their place the practiced disciple discerns a continual succession of sudden manifestations only lasting as long as a flash of lightning...."[30]

At the foundation of Buddhism, then, is the view that the entire universe is arising freshly as a unified whole at each moment. Because everything arises or emerges along with everything else, this means that the condition of anything depends upon the condition of everything to which it is connected—and that is the totality of the universe.

Taoist and Confucian Views

Taoism and Confucianism represent the spiritual beliefs of about 6 percent of the world's population. They are the foundational religions of China that have also influenced Japan, Korea, and Vietnam.

The origins of Taoism are generally traced to the third or fourth century B.C.E. and Lao Tzu, a mythical figure whose existence is still debated. Legend has it that as the "old master" prepared to ride off and disappear into the vast China desert, he was asked by a customs official to write down his philosophy. In response, he wrote the Tao Te Ching—roughly translated as "The Book of the Way and Its Virtue." This book is the only written record of Lao Tzu's philosophy.

At the heart of Taoism is the understanding that the Tao is the sustaining life force and the mother of all things; from it, all things "rise and fall without cease."[31] The Tao is the source of all there is and so is the unifying principle that resolves all contradictions and opposites. Because the Tao is both everything and the source of all things, the Tao is ultimately beyond names, language, and thought. For this reason, it is called the "nameless way." The Tao is the "Mother of the Universe," a generative and maternal life force that continually gives birth to the universe. Because the Tao is regarded as inexhaustible and unbounded, it is empty of limiting characteristics.

The goal of Taoism is to live in harmony with the flow of existence. Life is forever moving, never still, always becoming, so the wise person learns to watch carefully and ride the ever-cresting wave of life's flow. Taoists see the universe as a vast ocean of interacting energy. Since they believe that *chi*, or life energy, is abundant throughout, great importance is placed on cultivating harmony in our energetic connection with the universe. By bringing an awareness of life energy into our direct experience, we see ourselves as participants in a vast dance of becoming, where everything participates with everything else. In experiencing ourselves within the flowing river of life, we can sense when we are pushing against the current or riding with the flow.

The second great religion of China is Confucianism. Its primary concern is the establishment of harmony between the energies of heaven and Earth. This religion was founded by Confucius, a sage and social philosopher who was deeply concerned about the troubling times in which he lived. Although his ideas gained little acceptance during his lifetime (551–479 B.C.E.), his teachings have deeply influenced Eastern Asia for twenty centuries.

Confucianism perceives life as a seamless and continual interaction between three realms: "Heaven" (a life force), "Earth" (the natural world), and "Humanity" (the socially constructed world). Confucian social ethics were intended to bring a harmonious interplay between humans, the natural world, and the forces of heaven through the binding force of the life energy or *ch'i*. This energy is the unifying, vibrant, and ceaseless vitality that underlies our physical reality. Ch'i is the life force of heaven that gives birth to the universe and nourishes it in a profoundly unified, interpenetrating, ceaselessly active cosmic process.

While Taoism and Confucianism are quite distinct in their specific teachings, they share a perspective of the universe that might be described as organic, vitalistic, and holistic.[32] They both see the universe as a unified whole, permeated with life and involved in a continuous process of transformation.

Indigenous Views

The indigenous or tribal peoples of the world represent roughly 6 percent of the world's population. "Native" or "indigenous" or "first people" societies are found throughout the world, and historically they have relied on subsistence farming as well as hunting and gathering. Without a written language, native peoples have preserved their rich knowledge of the world in stories, rituals, songs, and legends. Many people living in cultures with a written language tend to view the oral traditions of indigenous peoples as more primitive and less articulate. However, this is an erroneous perspective, as native cultures often possess an extensive and sophisticated language with a subtle and complex worldview.

Indigenous traditions observe an invisible presence throughout the world—an animating force permeating the universe and connecting all things into a living whole. According to Navajo tradition, a "sacred wind" blows through the universe and brings the capacity for awareness and communication with others. Our individual consciousness is simply a local part of this larger, animating wind or life force that moves through all of nature.

For the Lakota, who inhabited the upper midwest of the United States, "religion" is a direct experience of an all-pervading aliveness throughout the world. Luther Standing Bear, a Lakota elder, said of his tradition, "there was no such thing as emptiness in the world. Even in the sky there were no vacant places. Everywhere there was life, visible and invisible, and every object gave us a great interest in life. The world teemed with life and wisdom; there was no complete solitude for the Lakota."[33] Since a living presence is felt to be in and through everything, all things are seen and experienced as related. Because everything is connected through the Great Spirit, everything deserves to be treated with respect.

One of the denser concentrations of Indian populations in North America—the Ohlones—lived in the fertile region that now extends from San Francisco to Monterey, California.[34] The Ohlones, now extinct, lived sustainably on this land for roughly 5,000 years. Like the Lakota, their religion was without dogma, churches, or priests because it was so pervasive, like the air. Their religion was found everywhere, as nature was seen to be alive and shimmering with energy. Because everything was filled with life, power was everywhere and in everything. Every act was a spiritual act because it engaged the worlds of power. All tasks—hunting an animal, preparing food, or making a basket—were done with a feeling for the surrounding world of life and power.[35]

The Aborigines of Australia believe the universe has two aspects. One aspect is ordinary reality and the other aspect is the "Dreamtime" reality from which the physical world is derived. In Aboriginal cosmology, the everyday reality of people, trees, rocks, and animals is "sung into existence" by the power of the Dreamtime—and the Dreamtime needs to continue unabated if the ordinary world is to be upheld and maintained.[36] The Dreamtime for Australian Aborigines "... is an ongoing process—the perpetual emerging of the world from an incipient, indeterminate state into full, waking reality, from invisibility to visibility, from the secret depths of silence into articulate song and speech."[37] Like the Aborigines, the Kalahari Bushmen have a saying that, "There is a dream dreaming us."[38]

The Koyukon Indians of north central Alaska live "in a world that watches, in a forest of eyes."[39] They believe wherever we are, we are never truly alone because the surroundings, no matter how remote, are aware of our presence and must be treated with respect. A clear theme emerges: Indigenous peoples have long recognized the aliveness at the foundation of the universe. They understand that we are not, and never have been, disconnected from the larger universe. With a cosmology of a living universe, a shining miracle exists everywhere. There are no empty places in the world. Everywhere there is life, both visible and invisible. All of reality is infused with a vital presence and this creates a profound relatedness among all things.

Western Views

Although not a religion, Western thought is an integral part of the world's wisdom and has had an enormous impact on human development. Here again we find the idea of a living universe running like a bright thread through the complex tapestry that is Western thought. More than 2,000 years ago, the philosopher Plotinus declared, "This universe is a single living being embracing all living beings within it."[40] In a similar manner, the ancient Greek philosopher and mystic Heraclitus said of the universe that "everything flows, nothing stands still." "All things are in a state of flux," he wrote, and "Reality is a condition of unrest."[41] Heraclitus also declared that, "For those who are awake the cosmos is one."[42] He wrote that life is an eternal becoming and the universe is continually "flowering into deity."[43]

Giordano Bruno (1548–1600 c.e.) was a visionary priest and philosopher. He maintained that a spiritual force is found in all things, and that even the most minute body contains a sufficient portion of spirit to animate itself. Bruno felt that God was present throughout the world—a life force that permeated the universe and gave all material things some measure of life. No matter how small something might be, he believed it would strive to organize itself into an animated body of some kind, whether plant or animal. Bruno's views of an infinite universe infused with an animating life force was seen by his contemporaries as undermining the authority of the Catholic Church, and he was burned at the stake for heresy in 1600.

The idea of a living universe surfaced again by the mid-eighteenth century as the industrial revolution was getting underway in Europe and America. This revolution was accompanied by a new sense of dynamism, particularly in Western thinking. No longer was life anchored in the seasons, going round and round in an ever-recurring circle, progressing not at all; instead, life was seen as moving forward as an ever-unfolding expression of the divine. The philosopher Friedrich Schelling (1775–1854) wrote, "History as a whole is a progressive, gradually self-disclosing revelation of the Absolute." His contemporary, the influential German philosopher Georg Hegel (1770–1831), viewed humans as vehicles for the universe to become conscious of itself. In Hegel's view, spirit seeks embodiment in matter as much as matter seeks transformation in spirit.

Henri Bergson (1859–1941) was a professor who lived in Europe in the late nineteenth and early twentieth centuries. His writing powerfully expresses the idea of a living universe, infused with a divine life force that he termed *élan vital* and that animates, not only human life, but also the entire cosmos. He saw the whole universe as a pulsating, participatory reality. According to Bergson, the reach of our identity is not limited by our physical body, but extends as far as our conscious perceptions. Our body provides a manageable island of stability as we grow in our capacity for conscious knowing and expression of the life force that animates the universe. Beyond the power of our intellect, says Bergson, we have the power of our intuition, which is our connection with the "ocean of life," the cosmic vitality from which we draw energy and insight.[44] The "essential function of the universe" says Bergson, is nothing less than "the making of gods"—or human beings who are fully conscious expressions of the *élan vital*.

The British philosopher Alfred North Whitehead (1861–1947), developed a process view of reality in the late 1920s. In his view, what we consider the concrete reality of the universe around us is, in fact, a series of "occasions of experience." The overall universe is the totality of all of these occasions and, because free will is inherent in the universe, each occasion is always different, new, and alive.

I have only touched upon Western views, but this is sufficient to show there has existed a stream of thought that, for more than 2,000 years, has regarded our universe as deeply alive. In contemporary Western philosophy, this view is sometimes called *pantheism,* meaning that a divine life force both pervades the world and extends beyond it. This life force is both immanent and transcendent—including all that is in our universe and extending infinitely beyond.

Harvesting the Wisdom of Human Experience

Harvesting the wisdom of human experience is like watching a picture gradually come into focus and seeing an extraordinary image of the universe emerging before our eyes. There are common streams of experience being described by wisdom traditions around the world. Within each major tradition—Christian, Jewish, Muslim, Hindu, Buddhist, Taoist, Confucian, Indigenous, and more—we can find remarkably similar descriptions of the universe and the life force that pervades it: *Christians and Jews* affirming that God is not separate from this world but continuously creates it anew, so that we live, move, and have our being in God; *Muslims* declaring that the entire universe is continually coming into being, and that each moment is a new "occasion" for Allah to create the universe; *Hindus* proclaiming that the entire universe is a single body that is being continually danced into creation by a divine life force or Brahman; *Buddhists* stating that the entire universe arises freshly at every moment in an unceasing flow of interdependent, co-origination where everything depends upon everything else; *Taoists* stating that the Tao is the "Mother of the Universe," the inexhaustible source from which all things rise and fall without ceasing; *Confucians* describing our universe as a unified and interpenetrating whole that is sustained and nourished by the vitality of the life force or *ch'i*; *Indigenous peoples* declaring that an animating wind or life force blows through all things in the world and there is aliveness and sacred power everywhere; and a stream of *Western thinkers* portraying the universe as a single, living creature that is continually regenerated and is evolving toward higher levels of complexity and consciousness. Overall, beneath the differences in language, a common reality is being described—our life is part of a larger life.

Despite humanity's great diversity and historical differences, when the world's wisdom traditions penetrate into the experiential depths of existence, a common understanding emerges that is in accord with insights from science. This understanding is utterly stunning: We live within a living universe that arises, moment-by-moment, as a unified whole. The universe is a living entity that is continuously sustained by the flow-through of phenomenal amounts of energy in an unutterably vast and intensely alive process of awesome precision and power. We are beings the universe inhabits as much as we are beings who inhabit the universe. The unity of existence is not an experience to be created; rather, it is an always-manifesting condition waiting to be appreciated and welcomed into awareness. The "power of now" derives from the fact that the entire universe arises in the Now as an extremely precise flow. When we are in the now, we are riding the wave of continuous creation. Each moment is a fresh formation of the universe, emerging seamlessly and flawlessly.

We still have further to go in this inquiry—as far as we can possibly open in our imagination and experience. We have seen that the visible universe is only the smallest fraction of the known universe. We have also seen that our universe emerged from "nothing" roughly 14 billion years ago and is sustained by stupendous energies, moment-by-moment. The understanding that most of our universe is invisible and all of it continuously emerges from nothing visible points to the existence of an extraordinarily powerful, generative ground. We turn to explore the infinite beyond our universe, the deep context that gave birth to and sustains our cosmos—the

"Meta Universe" (as described by many scientists) and the "Mother Universe" (as described by many wisdom traditions). In the following chapter, I speak of the "Mother Universe," but what is being described is beyond words or concepts and beyond the space and time of our particular universe. The Mother Universe is nothing other than the infinitely subtle and creative ocean of aliveness in which we are immersed.

Chapter 4

The Mother Universe

We bear the universe in our being as the universe bears us in its being.
The two have a total presence to each other and to that deeper mystery
out of which both the universe and ourselves have emerged.
—THOMAS BERRY[1]

Reflecting on the birth of our universe from nothing nearly 14 billion years ago leads us immediately into the depths. When we further contemplate that creation did not end with the Big Bang, but is a continuing process that even now sustains the entire universe, we are led into the realm of wonder and awe. How amazing: An invisible life force is creating our universe and then holding it within its spacious embrace for billions of years, while growing ever more conscious forms of life that are eventually able to look back and appreciate their origins. This is an ongoing miracle of such staggering proportions that there is a natural tendency to pull back from a full encounter with it. Let's not pull back, but dive into the depths and explore the deeper foundations of our existence.

What is the reach of our aliveness? How far and how deep do

we extend? Might our aliveness connect with an even deeper ecology of aliveness within and beyond us? When we look through the double lens of science and spirituality, what answers come back about this foundational question?

It is helpful at the outset to acknowledge that, historically, we humans have been extremely self-centered. Until recently, we thought the *entire* universe revolved around us! So, it is an exercise in humility to ask: If the universe is a unified, living entity, then what is the larger context within which it exists? Where is our relatively young cosmos located? Although we encountered the grandeur of our living universe in the previous chapter, here we open into an even greater immensity and ask: What is the nature of the generative ground that is able to hold and sustain multiple universes? This is much more than a conceptual question because we are not separate from this spacious context, but live within it and are an integral part of it.

The Meta-Universe in Science

When our universe blossomed into existence from an area smaller than a pinpoint nearly 14 billion years ago, it emerged out of somewhere. In reflecting on this, mainstream scientists such as astronomer Carl Sagan have put forth the increasingly accepted view that our universe "may be one of a very large number, perhaps an infinite number, of separate closed-off universes."[2]

Modern physics is now actively exploring the nature of the generative ground that is at the foundation of our universe and, likely, countless others. As I noted earlier, scientists consider space to be the basic building block of reality. The distinguished Princeton physicist John Wheeler agrees, and explains that material things are "composed of nothing but space itself, pure fluctuating space…that is changing, dynamic, altering from moment to moment." Wheeler goes on to say that "Of course, what space itself is built out of is the next question…. The stage on which the space of the universe moves is certainly not space itself…. The arena must be larger: *superspace*… [which is endowed] with an infinite number of dimensions."[3] What Wheeler calls superspace, other scientists have called the "Meta-Universe" and "Multiverse." I call it the Mother Universe.

We can glimpse the Mother Universe and her great power when we recall the enormous energies required to generate and sustain our universe. As mentioned in Chapter 2, empty space is permeated and sustained by unimaginably immense amounts of energy. If our cosmos were ancient matter floating through pre-existing empty space, then it seems reasonable that relatively little underlying energy would be required to sustain it. However, because the entire universe, including the fabric of space-time, is being regenerated at every moment, it is understandable that this requires phenomenal amounts of energy. A similar theme is developed by philosopher-scientist Ervin Laszlo, who has written, "The primary reality is the quantum vacuum, the energy and information-filled plenum that underlies our universe, and all universes in the Metaverse…. The universe we observe and inhabit is a secondary product of the energy sea that was there before there was anything there at all."[4]

From the Hubble telescope to the electron microscope, everywhere we see an astounding intelligence, refinement, subtlety, and design becoming progressively manifest. What is the nature of the deeper container that can hold this intensity and refinement of consciousness and creativity as well as our expanding universe? Many cosmologists now hypothesize that an innumerable number of universes exist—all experimenting, evolving, and leaving their learning to their offspring universes. To reiterate a key idea from physics, a black hole in our universe can be viewed as a potential doorway or wormhole into a new, baby universe, enclosed in its own bubble of space and time. Then, as the newly born universe grows to maturity, it will produce countless black holes that lead to the birth of other baby universes. Whatever we call this larger space, cosmology now provides us with a context—a hyper-dimensional ecology—from which we can regard our universe as one among many unified, living, and growing systems.

The Mother Universe in Wisdom Traditions

Turning from science to spirituality, what do the wisdom traditions say about what lies beyond our universe? The idea of a superspace or Mother Universe whose transparent body extends into infinity and lives in eternity is found throughout the world's major religions. The eminent scholar Joseph Campbell summarized a core theme in the world's wisdom traditions, saying "There is a life pouring into the world, and it pours from an inexhaustible source."[5] All of the world's religions attempt to speak, in their unique way, of the unspeakable ground out of which the visible world emerges at each moment.

Except for gender, the idea of a Mother Universe is very close to the Christian biblical description of God mentioned in the last chapter: "In him we live, and move, and have our being .... We are his offspring" (Acts 17:28). The Islamic tradition also points to a deeper, generative ground as the source of our continuing existence. Recall that the Koran says: "At any moment, if God wills, the entire creation could sink into non-being.... At any moment, if God wills, the mountains could disappear and become as clouds vanishing.... At any moment, if God wills, we could be as if we had never existed."

In China, more than twenty centuries ago, the Taoist sage Lao-tzu described what is called the Mother Universe in this way:

> There was something formless and perfect
> before the universe was born.
> It is serene. Empty.
> Solitary. Unchanging.
> Infinite. Eternally present.
> It is the mother of the universe.
> For lack of a better name,
> I call it the Tao.[6]

Here is an evocative portion of what the Chinese monk, Shao, has written in describing the Mother Universe:[7]

> If you say that It is small,
> It embraces the entire universe.
> If you say It is large,
> It penetrates the realm of atoms.
> Call It one; It bears all qualities.
> Call It many; Its body is all void.
> Say It arises; It has no body and no form.
> Say It becomes extinct; It glows for all eternity.
> Call It empty; It has thousands of functions.
> Say It exists; It is silent without shape.
> Call It high; It is level without form.
> Call It low; nothing is equal to It.

Recall from Chapter 3 that, in the Hindu tradition, Brahman is the supreme cosmic spirit and beyond the grasp of human senses, intelligence, and imagination: "Wise, intelligent, encompassing, self-existent, it organizes objects throughout eternity." Hindu cosmology views the all-pervading energy-consciousness of Brahman as the source and creator of multiple universes—an idea that is close to modern scientific thought. Hindus believe there are innumerable cosmic eggs, each of which is able to grow into a universe. Countless universes float like bubbles in an infinite ocean. This boundless ocean can be viewed as the Mother Universe.

The revered Persian poet and mystic Rumi spoke of the Mother Universe this way:

> The source is within you,
> And this whole world is springing up from it.
> The source is full,
> And its waters are ever-flowing.
> Do not grieve, drink your fill.
> Don't think it will ever run dry, this endless ocean.[8]

From Japan and the Zen tradition we have this appreciation of the generative ground from the monk Yung-chia:

> Like the empty sky it has no boundaries,
> Yet it is right HERE, ever serene and clear.
> When you seek to attain it, you cannot see it.
> You cannot take hold of it,
> But neither can you lose it.[9]

From Zen Buddhism and the Lankavatara Sutra:

> One Nature, perfect and pervading, circulates in all natures,
> One Reality, all-comprehensive, contains within itself all
>   realities....
> The Inner Light is beyond praise and blame;
> Like space it knows no boundaries,
> Yet it is even here, within us, ever retaining its serenity and fullness.[10]

Because our universe is constructed from and sustained within the life force of the Mother Universe, her presence is complete. There is no distance between ourselves and the aliveness that is the Mother Universe. We are that aliveness. The Christian mystic Meister Eckhart speaks of intimacy with the sacred this way: "God is nearer to me than I am to myself; He is just as near to wood and stone, but they do not know it."[11] It is understandable that this insight would have ancient roots in the world's spiritual traditions; when we become very still and contemplate our direct experience, we discover that we are not separate from the totality arising at each moment.

An Integrative View

What is the nature of the generative ground or life force that is able to hold our cosmos as a living system? Regardless of what the Mother Universe is called (God, Brahman, the Tao), all wisdom traditions agree that she is ultimately beyond description. Nevertheless, many attempts have been made to describe the cosmic womb that gives birth to and sustains our universe. Combining insights from both science and spirituality, here are six key attributes of the Mother Universe:

- *Present everywhere.* The clear life energy of the Mother Universe is present in all material forms as well as throughout empty space. The Mother Universe is the "ordinary" reality that is always present around us, the sea in which we swim.

- *Non-obstructing.* The Mother Universe is a living presence out of which all things emerge, but her aliveness is not itself filled in or limited by these things. Not only are all things in the Mother Universe, she is in all things. There is mutual interpenetration without obstruction.

- *Utterly impartial.* The Mother Universe allows all things to be exactly what they are without interference. We have immense freedom to create either suffering or joy.

- *Ultimately ungraspable.* The power and reach of the Mother Universe are so vast that they cannot be grasped by our thinking mind. As the source of our existence, the Mother Universe is forever beyond the ability of our limited mental faculties to capture conceptually.

- *Of unconditional love.* To experience the subtle and refined resonance of the Mother Universe is to experience unconditional love. An ocean of joy and love is her essence.

- *Profoundly creative.* Because we humans do not know how to create a single flower or cubic inch of space, the power of the Mother Universe to create and sustain entire cosmic systems is a miracle and mystery.

Contemplating these extraordinary characteristics of the Mother Universe is a way to awaken ourselves to the profound miracle of the living universe within which we are immersed.

Growing in the Mother Universe

We live within a "daughter universe" that for nearly 14 billion years has been living and growing within the spaciousness of a Mother Universe. The Mother Universe has existed forever, holding countless daughter universes in her grand embrace while they grow and mature through an eternity of time. This perspective not only transforms the description of the world in which we live, but also the way in which we regard the human journey: We move from a secular journey in a fragmented and lifeless universe that is without meaning or purpose into a sacred journey through a unified and living universe whose purpose it is to support, in freedom, the growth of self-reflective and self-organizing entities and communities at every scale.

Our universe and everything in it are expressions of the life energy of the Mother Universe. We are embodiments of the first miracle. We express directly the life force of the Mother Universe. Through our experience and learning, our celebration and sorrow, the Mother Universe also experiences, learns, celebrates, and grieves. We are sensing, feeling, thinking, and knowing beings, the living expressions of the Mother Universe. The Mother Universe yearns to give birth to her creative potential and, since her creativity is infinite, her creations will be infinite—including an infinite number of universes. The Mother Universe actualizes her infinite potential through our evolving experience. Our experience is her experience because ultimately we are nothing other than expressions of the Mother Universe herself. To explore this further, in the next chapter we consider the nature of our souls (or body of conscious-aliveness), which lives in the deep ecology of the Mother Universe.

Chapter 5

The Soul's Body and Our Cosmic Identity

Once the journey to God is finished,
the infinite journey in God begins.
—ANNAMARIE SCHIMMEL

A striking new image of humans is emerging: We are far more than biological beings—we are giants living in a universe that is almost entirely invisible to our physical senses, that is emerging as a fresh totality in every moment, and that is sustained by the flow-through of stupendous amounts of energy. Because the totality of our universe is being continuously created anew, we ourselves are being regenerated along with everything else. Cosmologist Brian Swimme explains that the intimate sense of self-awareness we experience bubbling up at each moment "is rooted in the originating activity of the universe. We are all of us arising together at the center of the cosmos."[1] We thought that we were no bigger than our physical bodies; now we find we are beings of cosmic connection and dimension who are part of the continuous re-creation of the entire cosmos.

The Size of Our Soul

To explore the nature of our soulful identity, let's consider insights from psychic research. As I described in Chapter 2, in the early 1970s I was involved in futures research at the think tank SRI International, reporting on changing trends and how they might impact government agencies and corporations. At the same time, in another part of this sprawling think tank, the engineering laboratory was conducting psychic research for NASA. Although I do not consider myself as possessing any special abilities, experiments at SRI gave me unique opportunities to learn about the intuitive capacities we all possess by being a part of this extraordinary universe.

Before participating in these laboratory experiments, I had assumed that my "being" was defined by my physical body and its ability to receive and send information (seeing with my eyes, touching with my hands). After nearly three years of experiments, with precise feedback from a wide array of scientific instruments, my understanding of the scope of my "being" expanded enormously. First, the remote viewing experiments demonstrated that we all can "see at a distance," receiving meaningful information through intuitive nonlocal connections. Second, the psychokinesis experiments showed we can all "touch at a distance," interacting meaningfully (and measurably, with scientific instruments) over a distance ranging from a few yards to several miles or more.

Through exploring these receiving and sending capacities in a wide range of experiments, my biologically encapsulated sense of self was subtly, though profoundly, transformed. At a deep energetic level I gradually understood that if my ability to send and receive information extends beyond my physical body, then my body is the gateway into a larger field of aliveness, a portal into a vastly larger being. In stages, I progressively discovered that the scope of my identity is equal to the scope of my conscious participation in life. These experiments demonstrated that we are boundless beings whose participation in the deep ecology of the universe is limited only by the scope of our conscious awareness.[2] *Our being is as big as our perception,* and our perceptions are constantly expanding or contracting, depending on our thinking. When we think that awakening happens only within our physical bodies, then the universe becomes no more than a passive backdrop to our lives that lies dormant, unexamined and unexplored.

This expansive view of myself did not emerge easily; I resisted what the experiments were telling me about the permeable nature of my self. Again and again, I found myself unconsciously invested in keeping a concrete, well-defined, bounded, and *permanent* sense of self. A harsh critic of my own experience, I did not come easily or quickly to the understanding that so-called paranormal abilities are actually completely normal. Only gradually did I release my primary identification as a physical body and open to my self as an energetic life stream — a being who constantly sends and receives in the subtle nonlocal ecology of a living universe.

In learning about the existence of psychic functioning I was also learning about its limits. The experience of receptive intuitions (for example, feeling-impressions about the well-being of someone we care about), are often vague, fleeting, and nonconceptual, even though they may be measurably real. Our expressive intuitions also have limits. Although we have the ability to focus our consciousness and exert a measurable influence in the physical world — as in psychokinesis — it requires extremely high levels of concentration and sustained effort. And I discovered that, if I entered an experiment seeking power over the measuring apparatus, my mindset generated a feeling of existential separation from the universe that was proportional to my intention to dominate it. While these experiences validated, for me, that consciousness is a phenomenon of the living universe and our identity is as boundless as our consciousness, it also demonstrated the universe has a robust and powerful ecology not easily moved or manipulated. We live within a complex ecology of consciousness, and as a living field it requires a subtle ethics and discernment to remain in harmony with it.

In exploring our cosmic identity, it is important to recognize our paradoxical nature. First, we are each unique, yet totally connected with the entire universe. We are each absolutely original; there will never be another person like us in all eternity. At the same time, since our existence arises from and is woven into the deep ecology of the universe, we are completely integrated with all that exists. Both unity and uniqueness are integral to our nature.

The second paradox is that we are both the observer and the object of observation, the knower and that which is known. We are more than thinkers who have physical bodies and a biological brain. We are also knowers who participate in a vast field of consciousness through our intuitive intelligence.

Third, we embody the paradox of being and becoming. The cosmos is continually arising anew and one aspect of our nature is the continual flow of becoming. We are also inseparable from the transcendent wholeness and great being of the Mother Universe.

Our identity embodies the three paradoxes of unity with diversity, knower and known, and being and becoming. Given the seeming impossibility of this, what can we do but awaken to the magnificent mystery of existence and celebrate our journey within a living universe?

Qualities of the Soul's Body

Our bodies are biodegradable vehicles for acquiring soul-growing experiences. Everything we think and do has lessons for the soul. Wisdom traditions suggest that, at the end of a lifetime, the lessons we learn are not remembered as conceptual thoughts; instead, they leave their unique signature in our soul — the essence of our being. When we leave this world, we take away the distilled knowing-essence of our passage through this life. If we have cultivated a life of cooperation and compassion, the essence of those life experiences will be carried with us. If we have cultivated a life of anger, mistrust, and fear, the essence of these experiences will be embedded in the resonant body of our being.

Because our being has the potential of immense reach and depth, it is very useful to have a firm environment to push against as we seek to know who and what we are. Our material world is an unfailing friend in the process of self-discovery. Imagine living in a world where the ground was made of sand. Because of its soft and yielding qualities, walking on sand requires enormous energy. Instead of pushing against firm ground to jump and run, we would sink into the soft sand, moving laboriously and tiring quickly. If all life's surfaces were soft and yielding, existence would be an endlessly frustrating, ambiguous, and toilsome struggle. We can celebrate the fact that we stand on hard ground and can interact with the firm surfaces of life — emotional, mental, and physical. These hard edges provide us with clarity for unambiguous learning.

Assuming we are here to discover our basic nature as beings made from invisible aliveness, the seeming solidity of the material world provides an effective learning environment to develop our capacity for reflective wisdom. Although we are created from invisible life energy, we may not recognize this to be our true nature. We are like clouds that do not realize we are made from the sky. It is a gift of this world to provide us with innumerable opportunities to encounter ourselves with clarity so we can discover the remarkable nature of our being.

Although our core nature is ultimately beyond description, four qualities of our soulful experience are recognized by the world's wisdom traditions and can be cultivated in our everyday lives. We turn to our soulful nature as a body of light, music, love, and knowing.

A Body of Light

Physicists have described light (photons) as the most fundamental, insubstantial, and free of all energies. Given the convertibility of matter and energy, we can say light is the most delicate form of material expression. Physicist Bernhard Haisch has written, "The solid, stable world of matter appears to be sustained at every instant by an underlying sea of quantum light."[3] The visible universe rides on the surface of this sea of quantum light. Physicist David Bohm describes matter as "condensed or frozen light." Light is ". . . the fundamental activity in which existence has its ground."[4] Because we live in a universe of light, it is fitting to describe the soul as a body of light that has the potential to evolve into more subtle ecologies of light after the physical body dies.

Light is a common theme in the world's wisdom traditions. From the New Testament we read, "God is light, and in him is no darkness at all" (John 1:5). Jesus proclaims the divine light within us, saying "You are the light of the world" (Matthew 5:14). When his disciples ask Jesus to show them the place where he abides, he says to them, "There is a light within a person of light, and it lights up the whole world." Elsewhere, in The Gospel of Thomas, Jesus makes an extraordinary comment that would have pleased Einstein, who saw light as a fundamental reality in our universe. Jesus said "If they say to you, 'Where have you come from?' say to them, 'We came from the light, the place where the light came into being on its own accord and established itself and became manifest through their image."[5] Jesus saw the universe as a place of literal light, and each human being as a light that came into existence from light itself. Jesus speaks on behalf of the light within the universe when he says "I am the light that shines over all things. I am all. From me did all come forth, and to me all extend. Split a piece of wood, and I am there. Lift up the stone, and you will find me there." In language appropriate for his time as well as for modern physics, Jesus was saying we are literally beings of light and telling "whoever has ears to hear" not to overlook this subtle but immensely important fact.

Gregory Palamas (1296–1359) was a monk and theologian who was venerated as a saint by the Eastern Orthodox Church. He put forth the view that it is through light that God communicates with the world. For Palamas, the physical light that illuminates the outer world is only a pale reflection of its deeper, non-physical radiance. Light is also filled with the *gnosis*, or knowledge, that provides inner illumination. By directly absorbing the wisdom within light, Palamas believed we could bring transcendent insight into our lives.

The idea of inner light is central to the Quaker (Society of Friends) view of the universe. Quakers believe that every person is born with an Inner Light and they sometimes refer to themselves as "Children of the Light."[6] This light can be discovered when we are quiet and look within. The Friends acknowledge this when they gather to work or worship together; they sit in silence and speak only when moved by their Inner Light to do so. When they glean a "sense of the meeting" from these inner promptings of the community, then action may be taken.

Jewish mysticism has ancient roots, and the Kabbalah is the body of oral teachings and texts that describe the direct experience of God. The most common metaphor with which the Kabbalah speaks of the divine is "light without end."[7] Before this world came into being, the "light without end" was present everywhere. Not only does the Kabbalah view the universe as a creation of divine light but it also views light as the carrier of consciousness. Consciousness permeates the universe, and human consciousness is a part of the larger field of divine consciousness and light.

Islam also celebrates the mysteries and splendor of light. In the Koran we read "God is the Light of heaven and earth" (24:35). Islamic sages taught that an inner light is contained within the visible luminosity of physical light. This "light in itself" or "Light of Lights" derives from a deeper, unnamable source; it not only makes things visible, it also makes them knowable.[8] The Sufi poet Rumi expresses this beautifully.

The lamps are different,
but the Light is the same.
One matter, one energy, one Light, one Light-mind,
endlessly emanating all things.[9]

In Buddhism, awakening experiences are often described with phrases such as "enlightenment," "self-illuminating awareness," "seeing the light," and "self-luminous recognition without thought." Buddhists also speak of a "clear light" (*Prabhasvara*) infused with wisdom, love, and creative power that permeates the universe with its shimmering presence. The clear light that infuses and sustains everything is a luminous presence, outwardly transparent and inwardly permeated with qualities such as openness and joy. The luminous energy at the foundation of reality is sometimes described as the "mother clear light." The luminous awareness we realize in meditation is sometimes called the "offspring clear light" or "child of the clear light."[10]

Other spiritual traditions also describe a light that infuses the world with both physical illumination and wisdom. In the Tao Te Ching, the sacred text of Taoism, we find the following passage describing the way of a wise person: ". . . the sage is devoted to the salvation of all human beings, without rejecting anyone. He is dedicated to saving things, without abandoning anything. This is the practice of the clear light."

The revered poet Walt Whitman wrote about the colorless light at the foundations of reality: "ineffable light—light rare, untellable, lighting the very light—beyond all signs, descriptions, and languages." In seeing this light at the foundation of all things, Whitman said he knew the universe did not consist of dead matter but was entirely alive. Andrew Harvey, a contemporary religious scholar and mystic, writes: "Divine Light is what is animating this universe. Light is what is creating everything. . . . Everything that we are, everything that we see, everything that we know is the Light dancing and playing—the Light knowing itself in a thousand different disguises."[11]

When reading these many descriptions of the nurturing "light within light," I am again reminded of lying on the living room floor of our farmhouse as a child and absorbing the changing textures of light's loving presence. If we look gently at the ordinary things in life—a piece of tile on a floor, the surface of a desk—and don't press upon them with our seeing but simply receive what is before us patiently and with soft eyes, we can sometimes see an infusing and permeating clear light—a dancing liquid of delicate, transparent luminosity. Like heat waves rising from the Earth in the summer, although faint and insubstantial, we can discern delicate, rippling, shimmering waves of light that are the source and womb of material existence. We live within a field that is thick with energy and aliveness. If we overlook the fabric of seemingly empty space—if we look through it as transparency and do not consciously see into it with soft and welcoming eyes—we can overlook the aliveness at the foundations of existence.

All of the world's wisdom traditions point to the presence of a clear light infusing the universe that, although subtle and difficult to discern, is glowing with aliveness. The clear light of the Mother Universe is an ocean of intelligent luminosity that is not "in-visible" but "trans-visible" because it is far more than simple nothingness. The light of the Mother Universe is clear because it is unlimited and unbounded—and therefore completely lacking in obstruction. Because this clear light is the source and foundation of everything in our universe, it cannot be limited within the confines of our contracted world and so presents itself as transparent. Despite its transparent nature, this luminous and living presence has been recognized, tasted, and celebrated by sages throughout history.

A Body of Music

The universe is a single, extraordinarily complex, pattern of resonance. The world looks solid and concrete but upon close inspection solidity breaks down, and material reality becomes a vast ocean of vibrations, frequencies, and harmonies that converge, moment by moment, to produce the stable reality around us. Everything that exists—from atoms to humans to galaxies—has its "songline" or unique orchestration that contributes to the whole. We are made from music. To say we are a body of music isn't just poetic; it is also true.

Physicists are now exploring the foundations of physical reality with what is called string theory. Despite its shortcomings, it is giving us a new way to picture matter. In this theory, matter is no longer seen as tiny, solid points or particles; instead, the particle nature of matter gives way to unimaginably small, vibrating loops of nonmaterial strings. These loops of energy vibrate like violin strings and different vibrations are thought to generate different patterns that manifest as unique energy-particles.

Given that resonance and vibration are fundamental to the universe, it is understandable that we would each embody a unique hum of being that is recognizable to others as they experience the feeling-tone of our soul. Different temperaments and personalities naturally express a unique symphony of knowing-resonance.

Returning to the cosmic scale, many spiritual traditions portray our universe as being sung into existence. In the Bible, we read "In the beginning was the Word, and the Word was with God, and the Word was God Himself" (John 1:1). It has been suggested that the Word is the vast primal sound of creation itself.

From the Islamic tradition, the Sufi poet Kabir who lived in India (1398–1448) spoke of the music of creation in his ecstatic poem "Sound":[12]

> The flute of interior time is played whether we hear it or not,
> What we mean by "love" is its sound coming in.
> When love hits the farthest edge of excess, it reaches a wisdom.
> And the fragrance of that knowledge!

It penetrates our thick bodies,

It goes through walls—

Its network of notes has a structure as if a million suns were
arranged inside.

This tune has truth in it.

Where else have you heard a sound like this?

The ancient Hindu Vedas (scriptures) tell us that in the beginning
was Brahman, the Absolute reality. Brahman is often portrayed as
the great sound that gives birth to entire universes. Here music is
viewed as the divine thread that connects the individual soul with
the Supreme Soul of the universe. Brahman manifests everything in
the universe as vibrations, from the smallest to the largest. Physical
forms are thus sound forms. Music can help us to spiritually awaken
to the resonant soul of the universe. For many Hindus, the primal
sound of creation—the "sound body" of Brahman—is embodied
in the word *OM*, the sacred sound of the Mother Universe that
evokes her core qualities.

Chinese Taoist stories speak of the "Great Tone of Nature" and,
in Indigenous cultures, the combination of chanting, drumming,
and dancing is often used to connect with the spirit infusing the
universe. Music provides a rich universal language for growing our
soul. In the words of Plato, "Music gives soul to the universe, wings
to the mind, flight to the imagination, and life to everything."
Beethoven said that "Music is the electrical soil in which the spirit
lives, thinks, and invents." In different ways, all of the world's wisdom traditions recognize existence as a living field of music.

We are all musicians of the soul, and the optimal condition for
any person or society is a high level of creative tension. Think of a
violin. If the strings are too tight, it will break the body of the instrument; if the strings are too loose, they will produce no resonance.

Only when there is the appropriate level of creative tension can the violin make music. Likewise, to serve our soulful nature it is vital that we find our unique balance between straining so much that we harm the instrument of our being or becoming so slack in our lives that we are no longer engaged in a dance of participation and discovery. To play the music of our lives, we must become skillful musicians of our soul, continually discovering the right amount of creative tension.

With careful attention to our everyday experience, we can cultivate the songlines or musical qualities we want within ourselves—for example, the tempo or pacing of our responses to life, the harmony or disharmony of our communications, the degree to which we improvise in our interactions with others or, alternately, stick to classical scores and behaviors. We each bring a different songline to the larger orchestration that is the universe. Our orchestration matches our character and consciousness and is tuned through our bodily experience, emotions, and mental qualities. We participate in a cosmic symphony as a vast number of individual songlines come together in a new expression at every moment.

A Body of Love

The vibrations of sound, light, and knowing-resonance at the foundations of the universe convey a feeling tone. When skilled meditators from diverse traditions reach into the finest essence of reality, to the very foundations of existence, they report a common experience. The feeling-tone at the foundations of the universe is not a gray mechanical hum devoid of feeling; instead, it is a subtle resonance of aliveness and love.

With love at the foundations of the universe, it is understandable that love is a core theme of the world's wisdom traditions. *The Encyclopedia of Religion* states, "...many great figures have argued that love is the single most potent force in the universe, a cosmic impulse that creates, maintains, directs, informs, and brings to its proper end every living thing."[13]

Christianity is founded on the understanding that love is the essence of God and that our supreme task is to cultivate our capacity to bring a loving presence into this world. "Whoever does not love does not know God, because God is love" (I John 4:8). "God is love, and anyone who lives in love, lives in God, and God lives in him" (I John 4:16).

The Christian usage of the term *agape* (selfless and unconditional love) comes directly from the teachings of Jesus. When asked what was the greatest commandment, Jesus said "'Love the Lord your God with all your heart and with all your soul and with all your mind.' This is the first and greatest commandment. And the second is like it: 'Love your neighbor as yourself.' All the Law and the Prophets hang on these two commandments." (Matthew 22:37–41). As we extend our love into the world, it mirrors the love that God has for creation. In the words of the fourteenth-century English mystic, Julian of Norwich, "We have been loved from before the beginning."[14] We are created from love for love.

Islam celebrates *Ishq*, or the divine love of God. This is also the focus of Sufis, who see the universe as a projection of God, whose essence is love. In turn, Sufism is often referred to as the "religion of love." The great Sufi philosopher and mystic Ibn al-Arabi saw God as the "Beloved" everywhere. Through our eyes, the Beloved looks out and sees the world and is ultimately able to look back at himself with love. God loves himself through his creation. Al-Arabi wrote: "God is necessary to us in order that we may exist, while we are necessary to Him in order that He may be manifested to Himself."[15]

Abu-said Abil-Kheir (967–1049) was another Sufi whose passionate spiritual poetry expresses his intimate connection with the Beloved:

> Love is Here.
>
> It is the blood in my veins, my skin.
>
> I am emptied of my self.
>
> Filled with the Beloved.
>
> His fire seizes every part of my body.
>
> Who am I? Just my name; the rest is Him.

Here is the wisdom of the Sufi poet Rumi with regard to love:

> Through Love all that is bitter will sweeten.
>
> Through Love all that is copper will be gold.
>
> Through Love all dregs will turn to purest wine.
>
> Through Love all pain will turn to medicine.
>
> Through Love the dead will all become alive.
>
> Through Love the king will turn into a slave!

In Hinduism we also find the idea of *bhakti*, which is loving devotion to the supreme God. This is not romantic love, but an unselfish, sacred love that wants only union with the divine. Tiru-Mular, a Hindu poet of the Middle Ages, sang: "The ignorant say love and God are different.... When they know that love and God are the same, they rest in God's love." When the love of the devotee meets the love of God, there is an experience of undivided union.

The Buddhist meditation teacher Jack Kornfield describes the unbounded love at the foundation of the universe in this way: "I will tell you a secret, what is really important...true love is really the same as awareness. They are identical." As we deepen our awareness, we find that love is our core essence—at the very heart and center of our experience. Buddhism teaches a path of compassion, where we see ourselves as inseparable from the overall ecology of life. A core practice in Buddhism is cultivating *metta* (lovingkindness) toward all sentient beings.

All religions recognize that a life force, whose essence is love, sustains and permeates all existence and is accessible to everyone. The Mother Universe holds us in love as, with limited consciousness and great freedom, we make the long journey of awakening. When we learn the greater our love, the greater our awareness, we further our evolution.

A Body of Knowing

Physics has revealed that beneath the seeming separation of things there is a deeper unity—a nonlocal connectivity to our universe. We live in a holographic universe in which everything is exquisitely connected with everything else. Everything is mutually interpenetrating. The world's spiritual traditions agree that by going into the center of our life-stream we tap into the flow that sustains the entire universe and this naturally has great wisdom within it. The wisdom of creation is directly accessible to us as the hum of knowing-resonance at the core of our being. When we relax into the center of ordinary existence, we penetrate into the profound intelligence out of which the universe continuously arises.

Because the universe is a unified system, it contains within it all of the conscious experiences of all forms of life. Understandably, to touch into the consciousness of the cosmos even briefly—to experience "cosmic consciousness"—is a profound experience.

Jesus declared "The Kingdom of God is within you." If we look within, we will discover immense wisdom within our direct experience. The "Kingdom" is also all around us. Recall Jesus saying in

The Gospel of Thomas, "The Kingdom of God is spread out upon the earth and people do not see it." The treasures of this kingdom are both within (the felt wisdom and love of the heart) and without (a divine presence infuses all of creation).

All of the world's wisdom traditions declare this world is infused with sacred meaning and knowledge. The direct experience of life carries its own meaning and requires no intellectual explanation. Playwright and Jungian analyst Florida Scott-Maxwell offered this wisdom when in her nineties she wrote: "You need only claim the events of your life to make yourself yours. When you possess all you have been and done, you are fierce with reality."

When we allow our ordinary experience of knowing to relax into itself, we find a self-confirming presence. When we rest in the simplicity of "knowing that we know" without the need for thoughts to confirm our knowing, we directly enter our stream of being. The nature of the soul is knowingness itself; when we rest within our soulful knowing, there is no distance between the knower and that which is known. In turn, the familiar knowing of the soul is experienced as an inexhaustible mystery.

Recognizing Ourselves Before We Die

When our physical body dies, will we recognize our subtle body of light and knowing-resonance? Will we recognize the unique orchestration and music of our being, the distinct way we light up the world with our luminous knowing? If we fail to recognize ourselves in this way, if we require the assistance of a physical body to anchor our self-recognition, then we are limiting ourselves to a world of three dimensions. The afterlife is unknown; however, the body of resonance, light and love that lives in eternity is knowable. Our responsibility is not to be concerned with the afterlife, but to be so fully present in this life that we recognize the familiar resonance of who we are, wherever we might be.

Many spiritual traditions tell us how important it is to be awake to our soulful nature at the time of death. What happens after we die seems likely to forever remain a mystery. However, if we do not become familiar with our subtle self while we have the precious vehicle of a physical body, we can fail to recognize ourselves when our physical body dies. In The Gospel of Thomas, Jesus says, "Take heed of the Living One while you are alive, lest you die and seek to see Him and be unable to do so."[16] Because we are created from the non-visible reality of the Mother Universe, we may die and not see that this is who and what we are. Our physical body is an anchor for light illuminating light, knowing recognizing knowing, and love appreciating love. If, in freedom, we have not made friends with ourselves during this lifetime, our physical bodies can die and the animating life energy of our being may dissipate and lose its coherence. We may then require the constraint of a material world to enable us to encounter ourselves once again.

Years ago, in catching glimpses of myself as a being of knowing-resonance, I confronted the stark question we are each called to answer: Will I recognize myself without a physical body when I die? When I asked myself this question, in truth, I wasn't sure I would. I had not made friends with myself sufficiently for me to feel confident that I knew myself as a body of luminous knowing-resonance. I was not yet adequately familiar with the music of my own being to recognize the unique orchestration I brought into the world. Looking beyond my short lifetime, I realized this unfamiliarity with myself would likely require further returns to our physical reality, so I would again have the opportunity for clear encounters with my cosmic Self. With this understanding has come decades of meditation and contemplation as I have sought to become a more intimate, soulful friend with myself—my own best friend who "I" recognize intuitively.

Why should we be concerned with recognizing the "Living One" or the eternal being within ourselves while we are alive in this physical realm? Jesus gives an important answer when he says, "In my Father's house are many rooms. If it were not so, I would have told you." (John 14:2). I believe Jesus is saying that, in the vast ecology of the cosmos, there are living spaces suitable for all beings. Another saying attributed to Jesus—found on an Arabic inscription on a city gate in India—makes the function of this world clear: "This world is a bridge. Pass over it, but do not build your house upon it."[17]

Buddhists also believe we must discover our subtle, inner nature so we can recognize ourselves when we die. They emphasize it is precisely while we have a physical body that it is important to recognize our core nature as pure awareness or as the "ground luminosity."[18] Because the essence of who we are is so subtle, when we die we can become confused, disoriented, and unable to sustain self-recognition. To keep from becoming overwhelmed by the sights, sounds, colors, and visions that arise in the passage with death, Buddhists teach that we must attain some degree of stability in self-recognition in the here and now. If we pay attention to the natural wakefulness at the core of our everyday consciousness, we will be familiar with ourselves at the time of death.[19] The Dalai Lama counsels that, because we don't know when we will die, it is of great benefit to be well-prepared as, at the time of death, the total responsibility for awareness falls upon us. He writes, "The body is compared to a guest house; it is a place to stay for just a short time.... When the day comes for consciousness to leave, the guest house of the body must be left behind."[20]

Turning from Buddhism to the wisdom of the fifteenth-century Hindu and Sufi master Kabir:

The idea that the soul will join with the ecstatic
just because the body is rotten —
that is all fantasy.
What is found now is found then.
If you find nothing now,
you will simply end up with an apartment in the City of Death.
If you make love with the divine now,
in the next life you will have the face of satisfied desire.[21]

If we use our time on Earth to come to self-referencing awareness, we will have anchored the gift of eternity in direct knowing. We can then evolve and grow forever in the infinite ecologies of the Mother Universe.

If the universe is non-living at its foundations, it will take a miracle to save us from extinction at the time of death, and then to take us from here to a heaven (or promised land) of continuing aliveness. However, if the universe is alive, then we are already nested and growing within its aliveness. When our physical body dies, the life-stream that we are will move into the larger aliveness of the living universe. We don't need a miracle to save us — we are already inside the first miracle of sustaining aliveness. Instead of being saved from death, our job is to bring mindful attention to our enduring aliveness in the here and now.

I do not view awakening to our participation in the Mother Universe as the end of our spiritual journey; instead, I believe it is only the barest beginning. As we learn the skills of consciously recognizing ourselves as flow-through beings of cosmic dimension and purpose, we are meeting the basic requirement for our journey through eternity. Once knowingness knows itself directly, then that knowingness can live and learn forever as a luminous stream of being in the deep ecology of the Mother Universe. *Awakening is never finished: We will forever be "enlightening" ourselves—becoming lighter so that we have the ability to participate in ever more free, subtle, open, delicate and expressive ecologies of being and becoming.*

When we die, we will not need to remember the material details of our lives because the knowing-resonance that we are embodies the essential wisdom of our lifetime of experience. In the words of the spiritual teacher Thomas Merton, "Every moment and every event of every man's life on earth plants something in his soul."

As we cultivate our capacity for mindful living we lessen the need for a material world and a physical body to awaken the knowing process to itself. If 96 percent of the known universe is invisible, then, when our body dies (the visible four percent), that does not mean that the invisible aspect of our aliveness dissipates and dies as well. Ultimately, the physical body that provides the structure for aligning conscious knowing will die, and we can endure as a self-confirming body of light, love, and knowing-resonance.

Once grounded in our capacity to recognize ourselves as a body of awareness, we can be self-remembering without fear of forgetting ourselves. When we die the full responsibility for self-luminous recognition falls upon each of us. Now is the time to recognize ourselves. In consciously becoming intimate friends with ourselves, we are directly participating in the life-stream of the universe and consciously cultivating the body of knowing that lives and moves within the deep ecology of the Mother Universe. At the heart of life is a simple task: to become intimate and forgiving friends with ourselves and to grow ourselves as a stream of light, love, music, and knowing.

Part Three

Where Are We Going?

Chapter 6

Where Is the Universe Going?

The universe is a single living being embracing
all living beings within it.
—PLOTINUS

Is there a discernible direction to the unfolding of the universe? If so, where is the universe going? How do we fit into its unfolding? Is our evolution as a species in alignment with the developing universe? To explore these core questions, let's first consider the nature and expression of life in the universe.

Life Within Life Within Life

At the foundation of existence is a pervasive life force—unstoppable, unquenchable, untiring, and forever manifesting itself. Not only does this life force burst irrepressibly into the everyday world and then tenaciously cling to existence (think of grass growing through cracks of a busy sidewalk) it is also found nearly everywhere we look.

Living forms have been found beneath the polar ice caps, in high deserts with no water, beside erupting volcano vents thousands of feet under the ocean, and in pools of water as caustic as battery acid. Communities of microbes have also been found more than two miles underground in pockets of water that have been isolated from sunlight for at least two million years, living only on the chemicals in the rocks and the water that was likely carried there by meteorites. Life presses at the edges of material existence at every moment and in every place, seeking opportunities to emerge and find expression. No matter how remote or harsh the circumstances, the life force will seek to express itself and to organize itself into some kind of sentient entity.[1]

The deeper we look, the more complex the living universe becomes. An exquisitely creative, inexhaustibly intelligent, and infinitely aware life energy is both *immanent* (present throughout the cosmos) and *transcendent* (present in ecologies that extend far beyond our cosmos). This life force is simultaneously *personal* (upholding the most intimate aspects of our existence), *impersonal* (sustaining all of creation with great freedom), and *transpersonal* (extending beyond the boundaries of the cosmic system we inhabit).

A core insight comes into view from the combined wisdom of science and spirituality. Life is both fundamental and emergent: It is the fundamental ocean in which we all swim and it is ever emergent as life-forms organize themselves into higher levels of complexity and consciousness. The *sustaining* life force is fundamental, whereas *surpassing* life-forms such as ourselves are emergent. The aliveness of the Mother Universe has given birth to and continually sustains our living universe. In turn, our universe is able to give birth to planetary systems that can give birth to beings able to look back at the universe and reflect upon the magnitude and mystery of existence.

Because consciousness is an integral property of the aliveness of the universe, it means that *everything has a consciousness or knowing capacity that is appropriate to its nature.* Instead of emerging only recently with the development of complex life forms, consciousness is a fundamental property of the universe that has always been present. Different material forms mobilize this capacity with modes of reflection that are appropriate to their material nature.

We are life-forms who live within a living universe that, in turn, emerges at every moment from the aliveness of the Mother Universe. Life is nested within life, which is nested within life. Instead of a cold, gray, and empty place, the world around us is thick with aliveness, dense with unfathomable life energy, and sparkling with immeasurable potential.

Growing Self-Organizing Systems

Assuming the universe is a completely dynamic living system, a core question emerges: How does the transparent aliveness of the Mother Universe enter into material form and manifest itself as coherent and persisting structures like galaxies, planets, and conscious beings? How can we live in a universe of flowing movement that nevertheless appears as the stable forms we see in the world around us? That, I believe, is a central project of our daughter universe.

Everything that exists is a flowing movement that endures, not because it has inherent solidity but because the life energy of the universe flows through it. Like an eddy in a stream or vortex in a whirlpool, all that exists depends upon the flow-through to sustain a persisting pattern. If the flow-through stops, the whirlpool or the eddy disappears. What is true for the fabric of reality is also true for us. *Human beings are not solid or permanently existing entities — we are flow-through beings whose very existence depends completely on the life energy of Mother Universe flowing through us.*

Instead of spraying energy in all directions and losing coherence, the universe is continually focusing and conserving its flow-through energy by creating self-organizing systems. Everywhere we look the universe is busy with one overriding project—creating and sustaining dynamically stable entities. Throughout the natural world, we see a recurring organizing pattern of dynamic stability. This form is called a *torus,* and has the shape of a donut. At every level of the cosmos, we find the characteristic structure and geometry of torus-like, or toroidal, forms. The torus is significant because it is the simplest geometry of a dynamic, self-referencing, and self-organizing system that has the capacity to keep pulling together and sustaining itself. By virtue of a reflexive nature that curves back upon itself, the torus has the potential to be connected with and "know" its own dynamics.

The accompanying figure shows six expressions of this easily recognizable form—from atoms, to humans, to galaxies.[2] The physical forms found throughout the universe are visible expressions of nature's evolutionary intention and direction. We see forms that are turning back upon themselves in a reflexive process—connecting with themselves so they can become self-possessing and self-stabilizing.

Because we find this characteristic form at every level of the universe, it shows that a fundamental activity and evolutionary intention is being expressed in nature's designs. Life is constantly seeking to connect with itself—to know itself and grow itself to higher levels of self-organization. A natural expression of this deep, evolutionary impulse is humanity's striving to fulfill our species name as the creatures who are doubly wise (we are able to directly experience

The Torus Found Throughout Nature

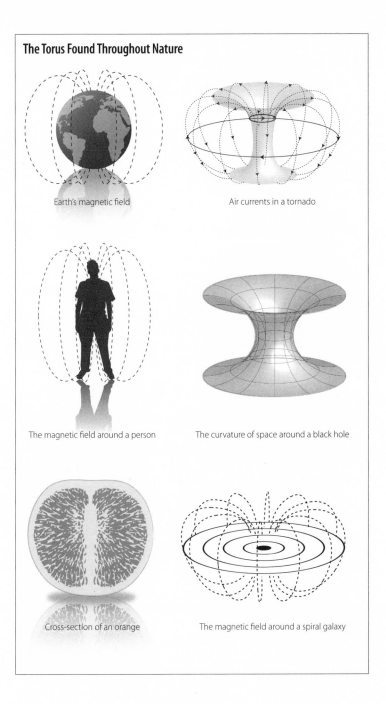

Earth's magnetic field

Air currents in a tornado

The magnetic field around a person

The curvature of space around a black hole

Cross-section of an orange

The magnetic field around a spiral galaxy

and be aware of our capacity for knowing). Humanity's efforts to awaken and evolve are a direct expression of the central project of the cosmos. In turn, we can learn a great deal about ourselves by considering the most basic properties of the self-organizing systems found throughout the cosmos.

- *Centering.* A self-organizing system requires a center around which and through life energy can flow. The center must remain open to flow if the system is to be healthy.

- *Consciousness.* A self-organizing system has a level of consciousness that is appropriate to its form and functions. From a capacity for primary perception at the level of atoms, to full reflexive consciousness at the level of humans, systems must be able to reflect upon themselves in order to be self-organizing.

- *Freedom.* To be authentically self-organizing and self-creating, living systems must exist within a context of relative freedom, as life-forms interact and affect one another in a co-evolutionary dynamic.

- *Paradoxical nature.* Self-organizing systems are both stable and dynamic (they are flowing systems that manifest as stable structures); both open and closed (they are continuously opening to the flow-through of energy and continuously closing into an identifiable entity); and both unique and unified (they are uniquely manifesting themselves at each moment while being completely immersed within and connected to the whole universe).

- *Community.* Communities of self-organizing systems are the foundation for life. An expanded scope of community supports new levels of learning and life-experience. Self-organizing systems grow in concert with other systems in a mutually supportive process of co-evolution.

- *Emergence.* We cannot predict what creative configurations will emerge as self-organizing systems grow to higher levels of connection and synergy. Smaller systems do not reveal the potentials that can emerge from larger combinations. To illustrate, we could not predict the properties of biological cells by looking only at molecules. In a similar way, we could not predict the ability of molecules to build cells by only looking at the structure of an atom, the building block of molecules. There is an extraordinary jump in aliveness at each level that could not have been anticipated by the properties of the previous level.

Where is the universe going? The universe is rolling out self-reflective systems at the local scale that are able to join into communities at larger scales that offer the opportunity for learning and creative expression in a context of ever-broadening freedom. If we want to go with the flow of our cosmos, we will orient ourselves in this direction.

Humanity's Central Project

If the universe is busy nurturing the development of self-organizing systems at every scale, then how does our journey of awakening align with nature's evolutionary intentions? If we fight against nature we are fighting against ourselves, and our evolutionary journey will be one of alienation and frustration. If we cooperate with the cosmos, we are serving our deepest potentials and our journey will be one of satisfaction and learning. Although we may not have been aware of it, the human community is on a path of development that is aligned with the self-organizing direction of the universe.

As mentioned in Chapter 2, our full name as a species is *Homo sapiens sapiens,* or doubly knowing humans.[3] Simply stated, this means we can see ourselves as objects in the mirror of our own consciousness. Being able to observe ourselves gives us an entirely new level of freedom and creativity. *If we use our scientific name as a guide, then our core purpose as a species is to realize—both individually and collectively—our potential for double wisdom or conscious knowing in a living universe.* As we awaken, the cosmos also awakens. This is what I have called the "great awakening." The cosmos is bending back upon itself as we humans cross the threshold of reflection and begin to contemplate ourselves within the cosmos. As the bending arc of evolution follows its course and consciousness returns to itself, we are fulfilling the potentials of the universe for creating self-organizing forms of life that are progressively ever more self-reflective. A simple visualization of stages of awakening follows. These stages are discussed in detail in the next chapter.

Does our development as doubly wise beings align with the universe's central project of developing self-organizing systems? As the figure's simple images suggest, I believe that *humanity and the universe are evolving in the same direction.* After billions of years of evolution, a life-form has emerged on the Earth that is literally the universe looking back at herself and her creations through the unique perspective and experience of each individual person. A gar-

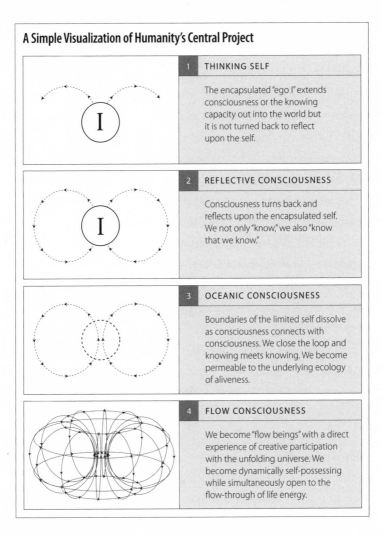

A Simple Visualization of Humanity's Central Project

	1 THINKING SELF
	The encapsulated "ego I" extends consciousness or the knowing capacity out into the world but it is not turned back to reflect upon the self.
	2 REFLECTIVE CONSCIOUSNESS
	Consciousness turns back and reflects upon the encapsulated self. We not only "know," we also "know that we know."
	3 OCEANIC CONSCIOUSNESS
	Boundaries of the limited self dissolve as consciousness connects with consciousness. We close the loop and knowing meets knowing. We become permeable to the underlying ecology of aliveness.
	4 FLOW CONSCIOUSNESS
	We become "flow beings" with a direct experience of creative participation with the unfolding universe. We become dynamically self-possessing while simultaneously open to the flow-through of life energy.

dener appreciating a flower or an astronomer peering out at the night sky actually represents the closing of a loop of awareness that began with the birth of our cosmos some 14 billion years ago. We are the eyes, hands, voices, and heart of the cosmos. Our universe gave birth to and sustains living planets, which, in turn, have given rise to life-forms that are now able to look back at the universe with wonder and awe. The awakening of a reflective human consciousness enables the universe to know itself and to experiment consciously in its own evolution.

We can see a fundamental principle at work in the universe: Evolution requires both matter and consciousness. Matter is blind in its evolutionary ascent without the mirroring capacity that consciousness provides; consciousness is blind in its evolutionary ascent without the grounding capacity that matter provides. Evolution is a mutually supportive process whereby matter seeks reflective affirmation of its presence through consciousness as much as consciousness seeks clarity of expression through matter. *The goal of evolution is not to move from matter to consciousness; rather, it is to integrate matter and consciousness into a co-evolving spiral of mutual refinement that ultimately reveals the Mother Universe from which both continuously arise.* Matter and consciousness support one another in their mutual ascent toward an ever-wider scope of integration and differentiation, unity and diversity. At very high levels of mutual refinement and dynamic alignment, the Mother Universe from which both arise is directly evident as non-dual or unified awareness.

In the ceaseless flow of our ever-arising universe, we are each a unique conduit for the aliveness of the Mother Universe. When we are consciously connected with the living universe, a loop is closed—"the broken pipe is repaired," as Tibetan Buddhists sometimes say —and the life force of the Mother Universe can flow through us and into the world embodying whatever qualities we choose to cultivate with our being and knowing.[4] Paradoxically, it is through our experience of unity with the life force that we also experience our highest individual creativity and greatest distinctiveness.

Once there is integration, once the loop is closed and a system is functioning as an integrated entity, it can move freely—there can be "liftoff." To illustrate, a tornado is a dynamic torus—a powerful self-organizing system with the ability to move while continuously holding itself together. Analogously, when we become fully self-remembering and self-possessing, we acquire a new level of soulful mobility and freedom. The physical structures of body and world that enabled our invisible consciousness to know itself will have then fulfilled their aligning function. As we acquire the ability to recognize ourselves in the mirror of our own consciousness, it opens the door to an infinite journey. With the ability to be self-reflective, the physical body that oriented our existence can ultimately fall away and the life stream of consciousness will continue to be self-knowing.

A grand adventure welcomes an awakening soul—a path of great compassion *and* great discovery. The natural companion of awakening is the compassionate understanding that we are intimately connected with all of existence and from this insight, a natural inclination grows to serve the awakening of all beings. Awakening also brings growing freedom as we see that our physical body does not bound the totality of who we are. As noted earlier, there is a growing consensus among cosmologists who think we live in a universe with many more dimensions than are visible to us. Are realms with breathtaking degrees of creative freedom beckoning us *if* we fulfill ourselves here? Because we have experienced the richness and complexity of life in the third dimension, what must it be like to have the spaciousness and freedom of, say, the thirtieth dimension? Just as few would want to stay in the third grade forever, I believe few would want to stay in the third dimension forever. If we become fully self-referencing beings and can experience "liftoff," would we choose to stay grounded? Analogously, if we build an airplane, would we be content to forever taxi down the runway or might we want someday to lift off and soar into the spacious sky?

A Garden for Growing Life

Two remarkable dynamics are at work. The first dynamic is often called the "universe story," and is the grand narrative of the universe evolving through time. The universe story portrays humanity as descendants of a vast creative lineage stretching over the past 14 billion years. The second dynamic is what I call the "great awakening," and it is the account of humanity progressively awakening to the miracle of the universe arising as a fresh creation at every moment. Where the universe story provides a stunning narrative of the "horizontal" unfolding across time, awakening to a living universe adds a further dimension: the "vertical" creation of the cosmos in time. The universe story focuses on the evolution of the universe *through* time and the living universe focuses on the universe being created *in* time. The vertical dynamic of continuous creation slices through all that exists and reveals everything as a single orchestration happening all at once. We are, at every moment, a part of this grand unity of creation. The first miracle—the flow of continuous creation of the cosmos—is so subtle and occurs at such a high rate of speed that it is easy to overlook. As we have seen, it is those who invest long periods in quiet contemplation and meditation—participants in the world's wisdom traditions—who have perceived this flow most clearly and described it most pointedly.

Our awakening to a new understanding of the universe in both its horizontal and its vertical aspect represents a stunning and extraordinary re-imagining of where we are as a species. Our awakening to the living universe goes beyond the history of any particular nation, region, or ethnic group. This vision of the human journey is big enough to honor the diversity of our past and to act as a beacon for our collective future. This is a story of such immensity and immediacy that it completely transforms the shallow story of materialism and consumerism. The emerging narrative tears back the veil of smallness and reveals humanity as creatures of cosmic dimension and participation. We are bio-cosmic beings who are waking up to find ourselves in a living universe and our evolutionary task is to grow into the bigness of who we are, both personally and collectively. Although the idea of a living universe has ancient roots in human experience, it is radically new and fresh as the frontiers of modern science begin to recognize how mysterious and magnificent the universe truly is. Humanity and universe are becoming connected once again, this time with the aid of science to cut away superstition and reveal the authentic mystery and subtlety of our cosmic home.

The evolutionary direction of the larger universe and that of humanity are aligned. We are not off course or on an evolutionary detour. Although we are largely on track in fulfilling our evolutionary potential, we now confront a supreme test of our collective intelligence and species maturity. Let's look at the challenging journey ahead.

Chapter 7

Humanity Is Halfway Home

. . . we are pilgrims together, wending
through unknown country, home.
—FATHER GIOVANNI, 1513

Where are we on our journey of collective awakening? As beings with an evolving reflective consciousness, how fully have we realized who we are? To answer that question let's move from the scale of an individual to that of an entire society.

Our journey of awakening into our living universe is not exclusively the journey of the individual; inescapably, it occurs within the context of society. With rare exceptions, our personal awakening does not happen in isolation, but is strongly influenced by the larger culture in which we live. Culture and consciousness co-evolve. It is difficult to step outside the perceptual paradigm of a culture and beyond the prevailing norms. Soul and society tend to grow together.

To explore our collective journey of awakening we can use the simple but powerful lens of one of the world's fundamental archetypes — the hero's journey.

Humanity's Heroic Journey

Because we are all living and growing in the same universe, it is understandable that we would awaken and develop in a roughly similar manner. We are all climbing a common mountain of consciousness, seeking higher ground. Although there are many paths to the summit, familiar routes and approaches emerge.

The themes found in the hero's journey are universal throughout the world and throughout history. Popularized by the renowned scholar Joseph Campbell, the hero's journey describes a path of separation and return whose general outlines are as follows.[1] An adventurer hears a call and separates from the everyday world to set out on a path of discovery. Along the way, the hero experiences many tests and trials, each rich with learning. Eventually, the hero confronts a seemingly insurmountable challenge that cannot be overcome with the capacities of the ego. The hero then successfully confronts a supreme test and awakens to a new and more soulful relationship with the Earth, the rest of life, and the universe. Upon completing this rite of passage, the hero vows to bring these gifts of insight back to the larger community and turns toward home. The ensuing journey is rich with additional discovery and learning.

Although modern media often portray the hero's journey as a quest for adventure, this is a shallow rendering of this archetype. Throughout history and across cultures, the hero's journey has been viewed primarily as a process of inner discovery and personal transformation. In going through a supreme test, the hero does not slay demons and dragons; instead, the hero surrenders a limited sense of self and awakens to a subtle connection with the living universe and the community of life. The hero's greatest challenge, then, is to slay the dragon of ego and the small sense of self. A supreme test devastates the ego and reveals the soul, enabling the hero to recognize his communion with a living universe. We can apply these insights to our "social ego" and see that, as an entire species, we are being called to a much larger sense of who we are and where we are going.

Looking at the broad sweep of our history, where is the human species on the hero's journey? The accompanying figure illustrates the evolutionary dynamic of which we are a part.

According to archeological evidence, we humans awakened to ourselves roughly 35,000 years ago. At that time, we had a weak

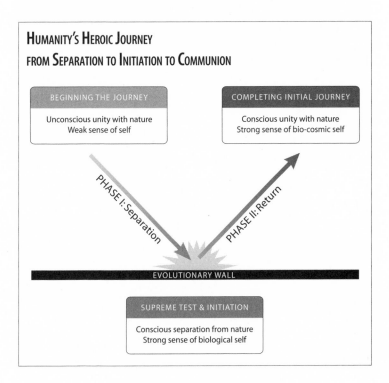

HUMANITY'S HEROIC JOURNEY
FROM SEPARATION TO INITIATION TO COMMUNION

BEGINNING THE JOURNEY

Unconscious unity with nature
Weak sense of self

COMPLETING INITIAL JOURNEY

Conscious unity with nature
Strong sense of bio-cosmic self

PHASE I: Separation

PHASE II: Return

EVOLUTIONARY WALL

SUPREME TEST & INITIATION

Conscious separation from nature
Strong sense of biological self

and shallow sense of self and a strong experience of connection with nature.[2] Over thousands of years, we became increasingly conscious of ourselves as distinct beings, but at the cost of separating from communion with nature and the field of life. As we move into our time of initiation as a species, we are challenged to reconnect consciously with nature as a living field while growing an even bigger sense of ourselves as both biological and cosmological beings.

This picture of humanity's journey tells us several important things. First, instead of a linear, one-way ascent of an evolutionary mountain, the figure portrays human evolution as pulling back from the universe in order to strengthen its sense of self. *At a crucial point, the entire process begins to bend back and consciously reflect upon itself,* which leads to our eventual return and communion with the universe at an entirely new level of understanding.

Second, when we look at the seemingly insurmountable problems facing humanity, we see the human species now entering a time of supreme testing. We are now in a pivotal transition zone; our challenge is to reorient ourselves toward communion with the cosmos and cooperation with one another.

Third, making the turn toward reunion with the living universe does not end our journey of learning and discovery. *There will be as much to learn on our journey of return as there has been on our long journey of separation.* This is humbling news. Instead of the modern era representing the culmination of human evolution, I believe that it represents only a mid-way point on the journey of realizing our potentials as doubly-knowing humans. *We are halfway home.*

A fourth important insight is also evident in this picture: *From a big picture perspective, the path of separation is the only path that we have known as a species.* Our history is a story of progressive separation from nature and one another coupled with the development of a strong sense of biological identity and ego-self. We have pulled ourselves out of our immersion within nature and grown into richly differentiated individuals and complex societies. As we make the pivot from separation to connection, it is important to regard the journey ahead with humility, and to recognize that we are all in new and unfamiliar territory.

Because the hero's journey so powerfully describes a widely recognized path of development, we can use this archetype to get a sense of where we are on our collective journey. Let's look more carefully at our long journey of separation, the supreme test of our species, and our journey of reunion.

Humanity's Journey of Separation

Humans physically like ourselves have existed for at least 150,000 years. However, our lineage almost died out about 70,000 years ago, when a period of abrupt climate change produced extreme hardship for our species. A massive volcanic eruption in Indonesia appears to have been the precipitating event. Sometimes called the "Toba catastrophe," this mega-colossal eruption—the largest in the past 2 million years—produced 3,000 times more ash and smoke than the 1980 eruption of the Mount St. Helens volcano. To indicate the magnitude of the Toba eruption, thousands of miles away much of India was covered with nearly six inches (fifteen centimeters) of volcanic ash. The resulting haze blocked the Sun, cooled the atmosphere, and triggered a severe ice age that lasted a thousand years or more and may have produced the bottleneck in human evolution.[3] Geneticists now estimate that between 1,000 and 10,000 humans in southern Africa survived this catastrophe. A few thousand humans who survived (perhaps from a single village or locale) provided the gene pool from which the entirety of modern humanity derives. These ancestors went their separate ways out of Africa to populate the planet. Now, 70,000 years later, their descendants are encountering one another once again—but this time as a family approaching 7 billion! What a remarkable story of survival and success.

Necessity being the mother of invention, the extreme hardship of this time led to an evolutionary leap in human reflection and creative action. It was in the years following this catastrophe that physically modern humans made their first great migrations out of Africa—first to the Middle East and around the coastline of India, across Indonesia, and on to Australia. Fifty thousand years ago, another wave of humans made the journey to the north and settled in what is now Europe. These two streams of migration eventually brought humans into North America roughly 15,000 years ago, and then on into Central and South America.

Stepping back, we can summarize our evolutionary journey in a single sentence: We awoke as hunter-gatherers with a revolution in self-perception 35,000 years ago, a revolution in farming and village life blossomed 10,000 years ago, the urban-industrial revolution began approximately three hundred years ago, and the communications revolution that is now enveloping the Earth began about fifty years ago. Let's review these major blocks of human experience so we can get our bearings for the journey ahead.

Roughly 35,000 years ago, we became consciously aware of our bodily existence and, with a *sensing consciousness*, we made a dramatic leap forward in our ability to develop tools, personal ornaments, and trading networks. It appears that we awoke from the numbing sameness of life to pursue a higher calling—a greater possibility in living that expressed itself in cave art, flutes made from bone, necklaces made from teeth and shells, burial of the dead, and more. In this call to adventure, the tests and learning were very close because life was experienced with such immediacy. Social organization was on a tribal scale, and our sense of identity came from affiliation with the tribe and our connection with nature.

Approximately 10,000 years ago, the last great Ice Age came to a close and we made a gradual transition into the agrarian era with its settled existence and small village way of life. A farming-based society with a food surplus and a *feeling consciousness* established the foundations for the rise of city-state civilizations. In this era we developed astronomy, writing, the priesthood, kings, warfare, and mathematics. It was also a time of widespread .illiteracy, superstition, and the oppression of women. Most individuals were impoverished peasants who had no hope of material progress.

Then, approximately three hundred years ago, advances in science and a *thinking consciousness* enabled humans to achieve unprecedented control of nature, and to bring unprecedented dynamism into the world. In this stage, people strongly identify with their intellect and grow in their uniqueness. A new sense of personal autonomy and freedom fosters greater citizenship in government, entrepreneurship in economics, and self-authority in spiritual matters. Empowered humans have been so successful in this stage that we are now devastating the biosphere and undermining our future. This is producing a planetary-scale, whole-systems crisis as the entire human family is pressed to come to terms with a new condition of the Earth.

The agricultural and industrial revolutions have produced the most differentiated, individuated, and separated beings that the world has ever known. While our journey has taken us as far from the Mother Universe as we will ever go, it has also taken us to the greatest degree of ego development—empowering us with strong identities as sensing, feeling, and thinking individuals. Because we are still far from completing the evolutionary project of soulful self-possession, the industrial era mindset can leave us feeling disconnected from the living universe (thinking of it as non-living), disconnected from one another (thinking we are existentially separate), and disconnected from our soulful vitality (thinking the soul does not exist). Our imagined separation is a source of profound suffering—and a powerful motivation to continue our journey of awakening to become whole with ourselves and the universe.

Because the culture and consciousness of the industrial era are so far removed from intimate connection with nature and the subtle life force, it may seem that this stage of development has been an evolutionary detour instead of actual progress. Despite the alienation and anxiety of journeying so far from the nurturing life force of a living universe, I believe we have been on a highly purposeful path of development. In the industrial era, we acquired our most distinct and empowered sense of self as material beings. Feelings of existential separation from nature and the universe were essential for us to realize our current degree of differentiation and development. Instead of an evolutionary detour, our progressive separation from nature has been integral to our learning and maturation as a species. However, our learning is only half complete. We are moving into our supreme test, which challenges us to change direction and reconnect with the living universe and the enduring aliveness within ourselves.

Our Supreme Test and Time of Initiation

Evolution moves forward on a bending curve and there is no going back. The starting gun of history has gone off, and humanity is moving rapidly into a new world. We humans have always been tested by adversity. However, our current times are unique in one crucial respect—and this makes all the difference. The circle has closed and there is no escape. Now the entire Earth and whole human community is at risk. Now the entire human species must deal with the reality of climate disruption (with resulting crop failures and famine), the dwindling supply of cheap energy, an enormous global population with most people living on the edge of subsistence, a massive wave of extinction of plants and animals, the spread of weapons of mass destruction in an ever more interdependent world, and much more. All of these are occurring at the same time the global communications revolution is making the world transparent to itself. Our supreme test is to grow consciously into this new world and learn to live in balance with the Earth, in peace with one another, and in gratitude with the living universe.

My estimate is that, by the 2020s, "adversity trends" will coalesce into an unyielding, world-scale systems crisis. Every major system in our lives—ecological, economic, political, cultural, psychological, and spiritual—will be in crisis as it is challenged to adapt to a dramatically changing world. This time of supreme testing will occur in a wired world that is transparent to an immensity of suffering.[4] This is a recipe for anarchy and chaos as millions (perhaps billions) of people will be on the move in search of a sustainable existence. With the largest migrations of humans in history underway, the likelihood of widespread civic collapse and tremendous violence will be extremely high.

Suffering will not be shared equally. Although every aspect of our lives will be challenged, not everyone is equally vulnerable. The world's poor will face greater hardships than ever coping with climate change and energy shortages. While energy shortages are inconvenient for the wealthy, they are catastrophic for the world's poor. Climate disruption, crop failures, and rising food prices create extra difficulties for the wealthy but disaster for those living at the margins of existence.

We are moving into a time of steel-gripped necessity, a time of intense planetary compression. In this generation, the world will become a superheated pressure cooker; the human family will be crushed by unrelenting forces so unyielding, and the stresses they place upon our world so extreme, that human civilization will soon either descend into chaos, or ascend in a spiraling process of profound transformation. On the one hand, if humanity is unwilling to work for the advance of all, then the world will collapse into a spiral of resource wars, and misery, poverty, and calamity will descend on the planet. On the other hand, unprecedented suffering may awaken humanity by burning through the unconscious denial, greed, and fear that now divide us. In encountering ourselves so directly and powerfully, a new human alloy may emerge from the furnace of these superheated decades. Our time of fiery transition may fuse the human family together with a new sense of identity and purpose that is strong enough to support the rebuilding of our lives to create a sustainable and meaningful future.

The challenges we confront are so great that we are called to move beyond our personal awakening to our collective awakening—as communities, as nations, and as a species. I do not view the emerging world systems crisis as a problem to be fixed. It seems natural that we would attempt to grow beyond the limits of the Earth to sustain us. Because nearly every organism works to exploit the surrounding ecology to the fullest extent, overshoot and collapse are common occurrences in natural systems. Since we have never before had the ability to exploit the entire Earth so completely, we have no experience in exercising global restraint. We learn through experience and, never having encountered an endangered Earth before, we should not be surprised if a great challenge or tragedy is necessary to awaken the evolutionary intelligence of humanity. However, once we collectively recognize the extreme urgency of our situation, the human community could awaken quickly and create a future of unimagined opportunity—or we could hesitate and drift into a future of unimagined tragedy.

The suffering, distress, and anguish of these times will become a purifying fire that burns through ancient prejudices and hostilities to cleanse the soul of our species. I expect no single, golden moment of reconciliation to descend upon the planet; instead, waves of ecological calamity will reinforce periods of economic crisis, and both will be amplified by massive waves of civil unrest. Instead of a single crescendo of crisis and conflict, there will likely be momentary reconciliation followed by disintegration, and then new reconciliation. In giving birth to a sustainable world civilization, humanity will probably move back and forth through cycles of contraction and relaxation. Only when we utterly exhaust ourselves will we burn through the barriers that separate us from our wholeness as a human family. Eventually we will see that we have an unyielding choice between a badly injured (or even stillborn) planetary civilization and the birth of a bruised but relatively healthy human family and biosphere. In seeing and accepting responsibility for this inescapable choice, we will work to discover a common sense of reality, identity, and social purpose. Finding this new common sense will be an extremely demanding task. Only after we have exhausted all hope of partial solutions will we be willing to move forward with an open mind and heart toward a future of mutually supportive development. Ultimately, in moving through our initiation, we can grow from our adolescent ways as a species into our early adulthood and consciously take responsibility for our relationship with the Earth, the rest of life, and the universe.

Humanity's Journey of Return

As we open to this new understanding of the universe, aliveness and awe return to the world around us. Where the existential mindset of the industrial era bleached the life out of nature and left a machine-like cosmos filled mostly with dead matter and empty space, the consciousness of this new era awakens the intuition that a living presence permeates the universe that—with equanimity spanning billions of years—sustains the unfolding of all life, including that of the human species.

Our return is not only to the Earth that supports us, and to the community of life that surrounds us; it is also a return to the living universe that sustains us. After maturing through the fire of our collective rite of passage, the human community can choose a path of learning to live in greater harmony with the Earth, peace with one another, and communion with the living universe. Ultimately, we seek to relax into the natural peace of communion with the totality—the Mother Universe. Recognizing this, we can look at everyday life in a new way. We catch glimpses of the interwoven fabric of the cosmos and our intimate participation within the living web of existence. Less often is reality broken into relativistic islands or fragments. Even if only for brief moments, existence will be glimpsed and known as a seamless totality. Touching the aliveness of the universe, even momentarily, transforms our lives. The renowned Sufi poet, Kabir, wrote that he saw the universe as a living and growing body for fifteen seconds and it made him "a servant for life."[5]

In this new era, we will regard the universe as the nurturing body of the Cosmic Feminine. Moment by moment, over billions of years, she sustains this cosmic garden as her offspring grow to consciously recognize and participate in her magnificent work. The Cosmic Feminine is not remote. We are immersed within, and created from, her body. We are She. Science strips away superstition and finds the miracle of a living universe. The sacred returns to the world.

The wisdom culture of the next stage is more ordinary and accessible to us than we may think. During the stage of the awakening hunter-gatherers, our ancestors would have been incredulous if someone suggested that millions of people could learn to live and work together in the manner now considered ordinary in advanced industrial nations. They would have been amazed to see us living in massive cities, driving cars on freeways, operating computers and television sets, and working in enormous organizations. We now take our urban-industrial way of perceiving, living, and working for granted. But, to the ancient hunter-gatherer who had yet to establish a village way of life, the thought of people able to function in a manner common to the industrial era would have seemed utterly impossible. In a similar way, attaining our initial maturity as an awakening species may appear unreachable; however, we seem to be designed with the capacity for successful realization of our species-maturity.

Overall, a key test of our maturity as a species as we move into this next major phase in humanity's evolution is how well we manage to integrate the many polarities that currently divide us. Unity and diversity, being and becoming, rich and poor, women and men, the eternal and the momentary, transcendence and immanence—the ongoing integration of these and other polarities will produce a strong and dynamically stable world civilization.

The Second Axial Age

The human family is making a pivotal turn from a long evolutionary phase oriented around a spirituality of separation to another long phase that is oriented around a spirituality of communion. A spirituality of separation is seen most clearly in what has been called the first axial age of religion.[6] The phrase *axial age* was used by the philosopher Karl Jaspers to describe the relatively brief period of time—roughly seven hundred years—when the great religions of the world arose: Hinduism and Buddhism in India; Confucianism and Taoism in China; and monotheism in the Middle East.

The period from 900 to 200 B.C.E. is referred to as an axial age because it set the orientation or direction for spirituality for more than 2,000 years into the future. Around the world, the axial age marked the growth of trading networks, the rise of large cities, and large armies equipped with iron-age weapons. This was also a time of extreme violence and widespread warfare. The response of axial-age religions was a countervailing revolution in spiritual growth that put compassion at the forefront.

The word *religion* comes from the Latin root "religio," which means to "bind together." During the long path of increasing separation and differentiation, the role of religion was to bind people, both to one another and to the sacred universe. People were not only leaving nature for urban settings but also, increasingly, disconnecting from the invisible field of aliveness. Here is a powerful summation of the first axial age by D. H. Lawrence: "For two thousand years man has been living in a dead or dying cosmos, hoping for a heaven hereafter. And all the religions have been religions of the dead body and the postponed reward."[7] As people saw themselves less as within the universe and more as separate observers of it, the binding role of religion became more important.

Historically, all of the world's great religions have understood that humanity is moving along a path of differentiation and individuation, and that a core challenge of religion has been to moderate the extreme consequences of our perceived separation. Despite great diversity of culture and geography, there is a common understanding in the world's wisdom traditions that is summarized in the Golden Rule.

As you wish that men would do to you, do so to them.

— CHRISTIANITY

What is hateful to you, do not do to your fellow man. This is the law: all the rest is commentary.

— JUDAISM

No one of you is a believer until he desires for his brother that which he desires for himself.

— ISLAM

Do naught unto others which would cause you pain if done to you.

— HINDUISM

Hurt not others in ways that you yourself would find hurtful.

— BUDDHISM

Do not unto others what you would not have them do unto you.

— CONFUCIANISM

Regard your neighbor's gain as your own gain, and your neighbor's loss as your own loss.

—Taoism

In happiness and suffering, in joy and grief, we should regard all creatures as we regard our own self.

—Jain

The heart of the person before you is a mirror. See there your own form.

—Shinto

All things are our relatives; what we do to everything, we do to ourselves.

—Native American

As you see yourself, see others as well; only then will you become a partner in heaven.

—Sikhism

Like different facets of a single jewel or different branches of a single tree, the human family shares a common experience at the core of life, and from this has emerged fundamental wisdom about how to relate to each other. In the first great phase of differentiation—a prolonged time of growing separation from nature, one another, and the Mother Universe—it was only natural that religion would become a vehicle to bridge or connect people back to the sacred universe. Therefore, a core message of religion in the first axial age was that of compassion—treating others as we would like to be treated. In a world of growing individualism and separation, religion served as the bridge between the secular and the sacred.

A second major phase with a very different axis is now opening before us. *Religions of separation will become religions of communion as we realize there is no place to go where we can be separate from the ever-generative womb of the Mother Universe.* At every moment, the entire universe is her revelation and celebration. The second epoch begins with the collective recognition that we are already home—that the Mother Universe already exists within us.

As the world moves into spiritual communion and empathic connection with the living universe we will see the role of religion differently: Less often will people look for a bridge *to* the divine. Increasingly, people will seek guidance and community in the journey of awakening *within* the living universe. People will want to know there are others on the journey of soul-making who look in the mirror of consciousness and confront their potentials for awakening and maturation. People will want insights about this journey from others who have been down this path before. They will want to know that there are guideposts along the way to support the awakening of their unique potentials. Less and less will people seek only religions of belief. Carried along in this great cultural project of awakening, we will increasingly seek religions of direct experience—religions of communion with a living universe.

Awakening into the Living Universe

We are moving through a great turn in human history. In making this turn, we are halfway home in our journey of return to a living universe. On the second half of this journey, we understand that we no longer require a bridge to the first miracle. No longer feeling a sense of separation, what we seek is not a bridge to the great aliveness but conscious guides within it.

All of the world's wisdom traditions recognize that if we are to experience the subtle aliveness of the universe it is vital that we consciously develop the arts of attention with tools such as meditation, contemplation, and prayer. Recall that we are giants in the cosmic scale of things and that it is easy for us to overlook what is happening at the more refined levels of existence. Happily, a literacy of consciousness is central to who we are as a species—we have a distinct aptitude for seeing ourselves in the mirror of consciousness. Whatever we may name our capacity for reflective knowing, the importance of cultivating this core capacity is recognized by every major wisdom tradition.

Throughout this book, the world's wisdom traditions have described enlightening or awakening experiences that emerge as we come into a more conscious and intimate relationship with the living universe. When our aliveness consciously connects with the aliveness of the universe, a current of aliveness flows through us and an "enlightening" experience occurs. At that moment, when life meets life, a direct connection between the universe and ourselves is realized and we have an awakening experience. We no longer see ourselves *in* the universe, we experience that we *are* the universe. Because the deep fabric of the universe is infused with its orchestration of qualities (light, love, music, knowing), we do not need to create or imagine awakening experiences. Instead, we only need to experience directly what is already true about the fundamental nature of the universe. Ultimately, when the conscious knowing of ourselves becomes transparent to the reality of our participation in an ever-flowing universe, we become beings of cosmic dimension and participation. Importantly, this means *awakening is not a process that is confined within the physical body and brain; instead, it is a process that involves opening to an ever more conscious and intimate relationship with the living universe.*

Awakening to the living universe seldom happens all at once; instead, it involves a demanding process of learning and discovery, often over a period of many years. There are three major steps in this awakening process that are recognized in different ways by all of the world's spiritual traditions.[8] Stated simply, our conscious relationship with the universe moves from *reflection*, to *communion*, to *flow*. The accompanying figure presents patterns of words to help describe the nature of these three stages of consciousness.

Let's consider these three stages of awakening more closely.

Stage I: Reflective Consciousness

Whether an individual or an entire species, the first step in awakening is to stabilize our capacity to pay attention by cultivating a reflective or witnessing consciousness. The word *consciousness* refers to our "knowing faculty"; therefore, to bring a reflective consciousness into our lives means to live in the mirror of our own knowing. When we are standing and talking with someone, we see ourselves/

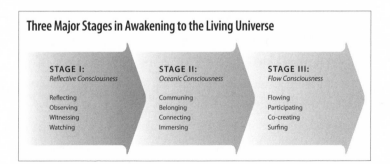

Three Major Stages in Awakening to the Living Universe

STAGE I: *Reflective Consciousness*	STAGE II: *Oceanic Consciousness*	STAGE III: *Flow Consciousness*
Reflecting	Communing	Flowing
Observing	Belonging	Participating
Witnessing	Connecting	Co-creating
Watching	Immersing	Surfing

know ourselves while standing and talking. When we are sitting and eating, we see ourselves/know ourselves while sitting and eating. This is a completely simple and straightforward process. We all have the capacity to consciously reflect upon and observe ourselves as we move through life. Despite the simplicity and directness of paying attention to ourselves, this is a very demanding and difficult task. We can easily get lost in the flow of our thoughts and the busyness of our lives. A brief moment of self-remembering is often followed by distraction and forgetfulness. Yet, with practice—with meditation—we gradually learn the skills of being present in our everyday lives. This is not a mechanical process, but organically observing and consciously tasting our experience as we move through life.

In cultivating our capacity to live more consciously, it is important to develop two qualities of conscious attention that balance one another—concentration and mindfulness. *Concentration* is the ability to focus on the precise center of our unfolding experience. *Mindfulness* is the ability to be aware of the panoramic totality of life. Concentration without the balancing influence of mindfulness results in the mind sinking into an activity, getting lost in the details, and losing perspective. Mindfulness without the balancing influence of concentration results in the mind becoming so diffuse and expansive that we feel "spaced out" and unable to be present within the precise center of the flow experience. With a dynamic balance, each acts as a corrective against the excesses of the other. Nothing is left out of our experience, as both the details and the spacious context of our lives are embraced in our consciousness.

Cultivating a reflective consciousness is a basic skill recognized in all of the world's spiritual traditions as well as in psychotherapy. All understand that the first step in awakening and healing is to simply see "what is." In other words, we begin by becoming an objective witness or impartial observer of our lives and telling ourselves the truth about our situation. Honest reflection and nonjudgmental witnessing are fundamental to both individual and collective awakening. In paying attention to our lives in the mirror of consciousness, we gradually make friends with our soulful nature and come to greater self-possession. The capacity for honest self-reflection provides a way to cut through the surface chatter of our lives and discover the deeper voice of our soul.

A reflective consciousness will bring a new tenor and feel into the world. Where the industrial era mindset with its "thinking consciousness" brought an aggressive, materialistic, and self-promoting orientation, a "reflective consciousness" brings a more receptive, trans-material, and relationship-building orientation; it represents a shift from masculine to feminine qualities. Embracing the feminine archetype (which tends to be more open, allowing, forgiving, bodily aware, and integrating) will enable humanity to move beyond the aggressive and competitive mind set of the industrial era and to promote the caring and cooperation that are the vital foundation for a sustainable future. By expanding the feminine archetype to cosmic scale, the universe is seen as a single living organism. Instead of an impersonal machine that is devoid of consciousness and purpose, the cosmos is seen as a living entity infused with, and animated by, a subtle life energy. Within this re-spiritualized framework, it is natural to view the Earth as a sacred, self-regulating organism.

Stage II: Oceanic Consciousness

The next step in conscious awakening occurs as the duality of watcher and watched merges into the unity of an integrated experience of conscious knowing. With stability of attention, the distance between knower and known gradually diminishes until the two become one in experience. We no longer stand apart from reality, observing it; rather, we come into a direct and unbounded relationship with existence. When we are fully present in the precise center of our moment-to-moment experience, we automatically come into a living relationship with the infusing field of aliveness—an experience that is intrinsically nurturing and satisfying. At the center, we find the simple joy and contentment of being alive. Our experience of intimate connection with all of creation naturally awakens feelings of compassion.

As we deepen into the experience of our communion within the seamless fabric of creation, it naturally awakens a feeling of compassion for the rest of life. We see that we are not separate, as everything contributes its part to the continuous flowering of the cosmos. Our scope of empathy and concern broadens as we are able to see beyond our own skin. Intuitively, we know that because we all arise from a deep ocean of life energy, a vital connection is continuously present. A natural inclination toward ethical behavior grows within us. Immersed in the larger ocean of life, we understand that if there is suffering anywhere on the Earth we are all suffering. We recognize that our experience of life is permeable, that our intuitive capacities extend into the ocean of our shared existence, and that we share in whatever measure of happiness or sorrow is being created for the whole.

We may momentarily forget the unbounded nature of our Being but with focus, intention, and grace we can take a breath, notice the warmth that arises in our hearts, and re-affirm our capacity for being in the world with lovingkindness. Once we *know* our cosmic nature and that we are immersed in this reality, we know how to look within to discover anew the cosmic aspects of our being. In a self-reinforcing spiral of development, we become increasingly secure in our knowledge of this ordinary miracle and grow as beings of cosmic dimension, connection, and purpose.

Stage III: Flow Consciousness

The third stage of awakening unfolds as we become increasingly settled within an oceanic consciousness and a feeling of communion with the totality of existence. With increasingly precise and sustained attention we begin to ride the flow of the universe as it continuously arises. Gradually we learn the skills of "reality surfing," riding the wave of continuous creation.

By embracing the full dynamism of the cosmos, the last vestiges of the passive observer are transformed into the fully engaged participator. The loop of self-knowing closes and the full capacity for "knowing that we know" is realized. By coming to the center of oceanic consciousness and great Being, we discover the flow of the living cosmos in its process of great Becoming. Being and Becoming are both true. To complete our learning we must learn the skills of movement, of flow, of reality surfing, of Being Becoming Being; we then discover the stillness within motion and the motion within stillness.[9] Enlightening experiences emerge naturally when attention rides the precise edge of the endless cresting wave of continuous creation.

What does flow consciousness feel like? Imagine you are riding a bike along a road with a 20-mph wind blowing directly at your back. When you are pedaling slower than 20 mph you feel the wind pushing from behind. When you are pedaling faster than 20 mph, you feel the wind pushing from the front. But at perfect speed—when the speed of your bike matches the speed of the wind—the world suddenly becomes very still and your movement along the road becomes nearly effortless. In a similar way, when our flow of awareness comes into precise synchronization with the arising of the universe, then the world suddenly becomes very quiet and our passage through life becomes calm and easeful. When we are aware of the stillness within motion, we are in the center of the flow of continuous creation. In flow consciousness, we experience a deep harmony as the personal and the universal move together in mutual synchrony.[10] Because any activity done with fullness of attention offers an opportunity to connect with the cosmic flow, this experience is always available to us.

No matter how mundane the circumstance, no matter how seemingly trivial the situation, we can always be aware of the subtle flow of creation happening within and around us. We can glimpse the current of creation in small ways—perhaps in the golden light of a late afternoon or in the luster of an old wooden table that shines and dances with an inexplicable depth and glow. We can also witness the buzzing aliveness of creation in places that may seem far removed from nature—a room filled only with plastic, chrome, steel, and glass will fiercely display the flow of creation in the raw. In the gentle contemplation of any part of ordinary reality, we can catch glimpses of the great hurricane of energy that blows with silent force through all things.

In learning the skills of living within a living universe, humanity will acquire the perspective, wisdom, and compassion we will need to sustain ourselves into the deep future. A dynamically stable and self-organizing planetary civilization can grow and become a participant in the unfolding cosmos. The dynamic integration of this stage represents both the completion of a long process of development and the foundation for a new beginning. We are making our way into the infinite reaches of our home—the living universe nested within the ever-sustaining Mother Universe.

In considering these three stages of awakening, it is important to respect our personal stage of learning and be patient with ourselves, neither getting ahead of ourselves nor lagging behind. For example, it is important not to reach for the spaciousness of a cosmic consciousness (conscious participation in the ecology of the cosmos) when a witnessing consciousness has yet to be stabilized. On the other hand, it does not serve us to continue to cultivate the subtle polarity of a witnessing or observing consciousness when we have developed the capacity to move into cosmic consciousness and achieve compassionate communion with the cosmos. We are each responsible for discerning where we are on our journey of awakening and for seeking guidance and a community of support.

Fundamental to our journey of return is resting in the amazing grace of a living universe. What a kindness it is to discover that we are her offspring. What relief from the existential anxiety of profound separation. A higher sanity emerges. Once again we can be curious about the invisible presence and look for the "light within light." We can listen for the great sound of creation as the universe arises silently in each moment and quench our soul's thirst with the sweet waters of the primordial ocean of aliveness, present since the beginning of all beginnings.

Part Four

Actions
for the
Journey Ahead

Chapter 8

Six Vital Tasks for the Journey Home

Take courage. The human race is divine.
—PYTHAGORAS

The human family faces a demanding journey. Because we are experiencing a systems crisis, everything is happening at once. How do we sort out what is most important for making our way into a promising future? Having pondered this question for more than thirty years, I suggest that the following six tasks are vital for making this unprecedented evolutionary turn to begin our homeward journey.

1. Co-creating our story of awakening
2. Cultivating reflection and reconciliation
3. Living simply and sustainably
4. Creating new kinds of community
5. Becoming media-conscious citizens of the Earth
6. Bringing our true gifts into the world

Co-Creating Our Story of Awakening

If we are separated from the universe, we are literally lost. When we don't know where we are, we cannot understand who we are or the nature of the evolutionary journey ahead. This journey is not a return to the past. We cannot go back to some nostalgic golden age of a previous era; instead, home lies ahead in a new relationship with ourselves and the universe. Chapter 6 described a great transition for the Earth that is already underway. On the other side of our growing systems crisis, the world will be a decidedly different place depending on our actions now. We will have either an Earth ruined through conflict or an Earth restored through cooperation.

At this pregnant time in human history we are each called to help birth a larger vision of the human journey. To respond successfully to climate disruption and the dwindling supply of cheap oil requires more than programs for energy efficiency. More fundamentally, we need a compelling story about the human journey that enables us to look beyond looming conflicts over scarce resources. As a citizen of the Earth, every person has the right and responsibility to contribute to the collective visioning of our journey.

The "great awakening" to a living universe is truly great. It is not a marginal or incremental expansion of the human journey; instead, it is a radical, deep, and powerful transformation. In our encounter with limits to physical growth, we are discovering the unlimited aliveness of our universe and the enormity of our growth potentials within it. Material limitation awakens us to non-material freedom. As one door of opportunity closes, another opens to reveal an immensely larger realm of possibility.

To establish a guiding vision for humanity based on the foundation of materialism—when science has demonstrated that 96 percent of the known universe is invisible—is to choose a paradigm suitable for only 4 percent of existence. The "4 percent solution" of materialism is profoundly deficient. The magnitude of the challenges we face calls for a "100 percent solution" that includes the invisible aspect of the universe as revealed by both exterior and interior sciences.

It is important for us to not get ahead of ourselves, but to recognize where we are on the journey of awakening. We are in a dangerous time of transition from separation to communion. We are between two major stages and moving rapidly into a time of planetary initiation. We are entering a world systems crisis and we must choose whether we will pull together in creative cooperation or pull apart in profound conflict. The coming decades will reveal the soul of our species and provide the opportunity for a rite of passage from one great trajectory of learning and development to another.

In this supercharged setting, a critical step in building a promising future is to visualize it together. Although many people can visualize a future of catastrophe and ruin, far fewer can imagine a future of opportunity and renewal. A future of conflict and suffering is easy to imagine, while a future of harmony and health is still a vague and unformed possibility in our collective imagination. We face big challenges, and it will take an equally big vision to transform conflict into cooperation and draw us into a promising future. To create this vision, here are four empowering archetypes that provide us with tools for collectively imagining a promising pathway into the future.

A Maturing Species

We could see ourselves as a maturing species that is going through the growth pains of a collective adolescence. Our self-image could be that of a young species gifted with many untapped potentials. We could see ourselves as immersed in the predictable turmoil of the adolescent years, testing limits and yet ready to move into early adulthood, where we are concerned with the well-being of the Earth and the future of the human family.

As I travel around the world giving talks about humanity's future, I often begin with a simple question: "When you look at the overall behavior of the human family, what life stage do you think we are in? Averaging human behavior around the world, what stage of development best describes the human family: toddler, teenager, adult, or elder?" When I first began asking this question, I had no idea if people would understand it and, if they did, how they would answer. To my surprise, nearly everyone immediately understood the question and their responses show that, around the world, there is an overwhelming agreement about humanity's stage of life—we are in our teenage years.

Although many people described our species behavior as rebellious, reckless, and short-sighted, many others also pointed out beneficial aspects of the adolescent stage of development. Adolescents have a huge amount of energy and enthusiasm and, with their courage and daring, are ready to dive into life and make a difference in the world. Many teenagers have a hidden sense of greatness and feel that, given a chance, they can accomplish wonderful things. Overall, the archetype of a maturing species explains a lot about our current behaviors and contains within it the promise of a hopeful future. As we grow into our early adulthood as a species, we can recognize we are an integral part of the living universe, consider the impact of our actions generations into the future, place meaningful work over pleasure seeking, measure ourselves by our soulful character, and patiently work to restore the Earth.

A Heroic Species

The previous chapter discussed the hero archetype at length. We could hold an image of ourselves as a pioneering species that is blazing an evolutionary trail and transforming a wild planet into a biosphere that will sustain life into the distant future. In this view we are on a heroic journey, moving through an unprecedented rite of passage and confronting the supreme challenge of building a new relationship with the Earth, with one another, and with the living universe that is our home. When we regard ourselves in this way, it seems evident that for tens of thousands of years, humanity has been on a path of separation — pulling back from nature and growing our sense of differentiation and empowerment as a species. Now our powers have become so great that they threaten the integrity of life on this planet and confront us with an unprecedented test of our species' character. If we move through this time of initiation successfully, we can make our journey of return back into a harmonious relationship with the Earth and the universe that is our home.

A Witnessing Species

A third archetype that provides a powerful tool for envisioning a constructive journey portrays humanity as a witnessing or observing species. Throughout this book we have explored the idea that humans are the most conscious life form on the Earth and possess a unique potential for reflective consciousness (knowing that we know). We are a reflective species with a distinct capacity for being awake to our choices and their impact upon the Earth. Empowered by the global communications revolution, our emerging self-image could be that of a human community that is progressively waking up and becoming ever more deliberate, attentive, and mindful of our way of living upon the Earth.

At a global level, the world is becoming transparent to itself—seeing itself as a whole system for the very first time. No longer operating "on automatic," the human family is increasingly aware that we can be conscious of ourselves—seeing ourselves daily in the mirrors of television, the Internet, and other tools of the global nervous system—and this changes everything. People in both agrarian and industrial societies are being rapidly enveloped in the communications revolution, with its capacity for a witnessing or observing consciousness. Whether we live in city, village, or farm, all humans are becoming "witnessing earthlings." Injustice and inequities that previously flourished in the darkness of inattention and ignorance are being brought into the healing light of public awareness. With the whole world watching, various kinds of violence—economic, racial, gender, religious—are being brought before the court of world public opinion through the Internet and mass media. The world is becoming transparent and this is having a powerful corrective influence on human relations and inclining our actions in a more compassionate direction. The archetype of a witnessing species that is waking up together is an empowering metaphor as we work to envision a promising future.

A Cosmic Species

A fourth archetype at the foundation of this book is an image of ourselves as the offspring not only of a living Earth but also of a living universe; we are the progeny of a vast, evolutionary chain of life that is regenerating itself at every moment. Seeing ourselves as descendants of a living cosmos, we can develop a collective self-image as beings of cosmic dimension, participation, and purpose. Seeing ourselves as part of the seamless fabric of creation awakens a sense of connection with and compassion for the totality of life. No longer do we see ourselves as isolated beings whose identity stops with our skin; instead, we regard ourselves as interconnected beings who are immersed in a vast ocean of aliveness. Every action is felt to have ethical consequences as it reverberates throughout the interwoven field of the living universe. We can tune into this living field and sense, as a kinesthetic hum, whether our actions are in harmony with the well-being of the world. As we see ourselves as the offspring of a living universe, it awakens a new sense of identity, ethics, and potential for the future.

We can use these four archetypes to tell ourselves a new and compelling story about the human journey. We are a *maturing species* that is entering a rite of passage that can take us from adolescence to adulthood. We are a *heroic species* that has been progressively separating ourselves from nature and becoming ever more differentiated and empowered, and now we are beginning a journey of return to the living universe. We are a *witnessing species* that has been moving through history half awake, not fully utilizing our unique capacity for being conscious, and now—aided by the global communications revolution—we are becoming more fully awake and choosing our path more deliberately. We are a *cosmic species* on a journey to reclaim our participation in the living universe. In seeing ourselves as a species of both biological and cosmic dimensions, we are taken beyond the bounds of the Earth and into the spaciousness of a vastly larger journey.

Combining these four archetypes, we can summarize the promise of the future in this way: *Humanity is on a heroic journey of awakening into the stunning reality that we are beings of cosmic connection and participation who are learning to live within a living universe.* Our potentials as a species are as magnificent and mysterious as the living universe that permeates and sustains us.

It is important for each person to feel they are contributing to the great story of our species. Conversation is the lifeblood of a robust and healthy society. One of the most powerful things we can do to strengthen and advance our evolution is to step back from the rush of day-to-day busyness and strike up inquiring conversations with our friends, families, work associates, and others. If we bring a spirit of authentic inquiry to conversations about humanity's future into living rooms, classrooms, and boardrooms, it will gradually awaken a new consciousness and level of self-reflection. These four archetypes invite us to ask: Are we adolescents or adults? Heroes or villains? Sleeping or awakening? Biological or bio-cosmic? As we get clearer about who we are and where we are going, actions can then come quickly and easily, where before they were paralyzed by confusion and conflict. There may be no more important task for humanity than to cultivate archetypes in our collective imagination that, together, can serve as a beacon for drawing us into a promising future.

Cultivating Reflection and Reconciliation

The paradigm of a living universe will foster a new level of ethics as people recognize that our every action and thought is woven into the infinite ecology of the universe. In his *Book of Mirdad,* Mikhail Nimay describes this insight beautifully:

> So think as if your every thought were to be etched in fire upon
> the sky for all and everything to see. For so, in truth, it is.

So speak as if the world entire were but a single ear intent on hearing what you say. And so, in truth, it is.

So do as if your every deed were to recoil upon your head. And so, in truth, it is.

So wish as if you were the wish. And so, in truth, you are.[1]

We each have the capacity to tune into ourselves and to know we are an expression of the living universe that manifests in a flow of immense subtlety and power. In our direct experience, we can consciously discern the subtle flow of the universe arising at each moment. We can see this dance of subtle creation outwardly, and we can experience our participation inwardly. As we awaken to the aliveness of the universe, the universe responds to us — the knowingness of the living cosmos meets the knowingness of a unique human. In the exchange, there is a mutuality of knowing that brings with it an experience of belonging to the universe and being at home within its immense community of life. We know the universe and, simultaneously, the universe knows us.

Discovering that we are an inseparable part of the fabric of existence awakens our experience of compassion for the rest of life. We expand our empathy as we come to see ourselves as beings of cosmic dimension and participation. The compassion we feel becomes the basis for a higher unity that transcends our great diversity — racial, ethnic, sexual, generational, religious, political, economic, and more.

A world unconsciously divided against itself while facing enormous challenges — and armed with weapons of mass destruction — is a recipe for global ruin. Without unprecedented initiatives for global reflection, reconciliation, and healing, our efforts to achieve a sustainable and meaningful future will be frustrated by the wounds of the past. Irrespective of differences in gender, race, wealth, religion, and political orientation, we all participate in the deep ecology of consciousness, and this provides a common ground for meeting, understanding, and reconciliation.

Reconciliation does not mean past injustices and grievances are erased; instead, by being publicly acknowledged and remedied, they need no longer stand in the way of collective progress. When injustices are mutually acknowledged, it releases both parties from the need to continue the process of blaming and feeling resentful; instead they can focus on cooperative actions for building a better future. Reflective consciousness provides a "place to stand" for bridging the polarities that now divide the world and keep it from working as an integrated system.

With a felt appreciation that we share a common foundation of existence, the human family can bring a spirit of reconciliation to these key areas:

- *Religious reconciliation.* Throughout human history, many of our bloodiest and most intense conflicts have come from religious intolerance. Reconciliation means each of the world's wisdom traditions is recognized and respected for its unique insights and contributions.

- *Racial, ethnic and gender reconciliation.* Healing the wounds of racism, slavery, genocide, ethnic cleansing, the oppression of women, and homophobia are essential if we are to shift the human story from conflict to community.

- *Economic reconciliation.* Disparities in wealth and economic opportunity between the rich and the poor are enormous and growing. Reconciliation requires narrowing these differences and establishing minimum standards of economic well-being that support everyone in realizing their potentials.

- *Ecological reconciliation.* Living in sustainable harmony with the Earth's biosphere is essential if we are to build a promising future. Because we are over-consuming the Earth, depleting resources, and destabilizing the climate, our future depends on establishing a new relationship of full integrity with the Earth's ecology.

- *Generational reconciliation.* Current generations are over-consuming the Earth's resources and giving little thought to the needs of future generations. Because our actions reverberate far into the future, it is essential that we reconcile ourselves with generations yet unborn who will feel the impact of our choices.

- *Species reconciliation.* Balancing human needs with those of other species is vital for our future. To maintain the integrity of the Earth's biosphere, we are challenged to restrain our impact upon the larger community of plant and animal life. Doing so will enable us to secure greater abundance for the human enterprise over the long run. Beyond restraint is the need to nurture our ailing planet back to health.

Deep wounds of the human psyche and soul will need to be healed if the human community is to live sustainably on the Earth. Without authentic communication across barriers of suffering and misunderstanding, humanity will remain divided and mistrustful, and our collective future will be gravely imperiled. Great personal and social maturity will be required for people to give up their resentment for past abuses and to make good-faith efforts to resolve injustices and heal injuries so that the human family can work together for its common good.

The first step in being healed is being heard. With the communications revolution still accelerating exponentially, the human community is just beginning to experience an explosion of conversation. Voices that have been shut out in the past can now be heard on the world stage. Martin Luther King, Jr., said that "injustice must be exposed, with all of the tension its exposure creates, to the light of human conscience and the air of national opinion before it can be cured."[2] Injustice flourishes in the darkness of inattention. When division and injustice are exposed to the healing light of public awareness, that exposure creates a new mindset among all involved. It may seem unwise to bring the dark side of humanity's past into the light of day but, until we do, unresolved suffering will forever pull at the underside of our consciousness and diminish our future potentials. When those who have suffered can tell their stories in the public sphere and be witnessed authentically, the healing of humanity's soul will be real. In bearing witness to the reservoir of unacknowledged suffering that has accumulated through history, we can release an enormous store of pent-up energy and creativity and achieve an evolutionary leap forward.

In the previous chapter we explored humanity's first axial age and saw that love and compassion have ancient roots. More than 2,000 years of history attests to the impact and enduring power of love. Compassionate sages such as Jesus, Buddha, Mohammed, and Lao-tzu all lacked wealth, armies, and political position. Yet, as the late Harvard professor Pitirim Sorokin explained in his classic book *The Ways and Power of Love,* they were warriors of the heart. They have reoriented the thinking and behavior of billions of people, transformed cultures, and changed the course of history. "None of the greatest conquerors and revolutionary leaders can even remotely compete with these apostles of love in the magnitude and durability of the change brought about by their activities."[3] In contrast, most empires built rapidly through war and violence—such as those of Alexander the Great, Caesar, Genghis Khan, Napoleon, and Hitler—have crumbled within years or decades of their founding.

The historical example of the ruler Ashoka, who lived in India 300 years before Jesus was born, is an example of the power of love in human affairs.[4] Prince Ashoka was born into a great dynasty of warriors and inherited an empire that extended from central India to central Asia. Nine years into his reign, he launched a massive campaign to win the rest of the Indian subcontinent. After a fierce battle in which more than 100,000 soldiers were slain, the land he sought was conquered. Ashoka walked the battlefield that day, looking at the dead and maimed bodies, and felt profound sorrow and regret for the slaughter. He immediately ceased his military campaign and devoted the rest of his life to serving the happiness and welfare of all.

Ashoka's thirty-seven years of benevolent rule left a legacy of compassion, not only for human beings but also for animals and plants. His decision to create sanctuaries for wild animals and to protect certain species of trees may be the earliest example of environmental action by a government.[5] Ashoka's works of charity also included planting shade trees and orchards along roads, building rest houses for travelers and watering sheds for animals, and giving money to the poor, aged, and helpless. An absence of war and an emphasis on peace marked his administration. All his political officers were encouraged to extend goodwill, sympathy, and love to their own people as well as to others. One of their main duties was to be peacemakers, building mutual goodwill among races, sects, and parties. Ashoka's compassionate rule established the largest kingdom in India until the arrival of the British, more than 2,000 years later. Based on the experience of people such as Ashoka, Sorokin concluded that love-inspired reconstructions of society carried out in peace are far more successful and yield much more lasting results than reconstructions inspired by hate and carried out with violence.

Again and again, Sorokin found that "hate produces hate, physical force and war beget counterforce and counter war, and that rarely, if ever, do these factors lead to peace and social well-being."[6] As the teachings of the world's great sages and the example of leaders from Ashoka to Gandhi and King attest, it is vitally important for us to bring reconciliation and forgiveness into our world at this pivotal time.

Living Simply and Sustainably

"Simplicity reveals the master," says an old adage. More than 2000 years ago, in the same historical period that Christians were saying "Give me neither poverty nor wealth" (Proverbs 30:8), the Taoists were asserting "He who knows he has enough is rich" (Lao Tzu), Plato and Aristotle had proclaimed the importance of the "golden mean" (a path through life with neither excess nor deficit) and the Buddhists were encouraging a "middle way" between poverty and mindless accumulation. The wisdom of simplicity is not a recent revelation.

As we master the art of living on Earth, our mastery will be evident in the simplicity of our way of living. Simplicity does not mean turning away from progress; to the contrary, it is an expression of a maturing civilization. We can gain insight into the relationship between simplicity and progress from the eminent historian Arnold Toynbee, who invested a lifetime in studying the rise and fall of civilizations throughout history. Based on his voluminous studies, Toynbee summarized the essence of a civilization's growth in what he called the *Law of Progressive Simplification*. He wrote that a civilization's progress and growth was not to be measured by its conquest of land and people; rather, the true measure of growth lies in a civilization's ability to transfer increasing amounts of energy and attention from the material side of life to the non-material side—areas such as education, cultural and artistic expression, and the strength of democracy and society.[7] Toynbee also coined the word *etherialization* to describe the historical process whereby humans learn to accomplish the same, or even greater, results using less time and energy. Buckminster Fuller called this process *ephemeralization* (although his emphasis was primarily on getting greater material performance for less time, weight, and energy invested).

We can see material ephemeralization at work in many areas of our lives. For example, computers have evolved from room-sized giants to slim laptops with vastly more computing power. Libraries are evolving from massive buildings that warehouse millions of books to small computer chips that can store an even greater volume of knowledge. The telephone has evolved from a cumbersome network of telephone poles, wires, and transformers to cheaper, lighter, and more powerful cell phone technologies that employ transmitting towers and get rid of the bulky, burdensome, and weighty copper wires strung across the landscape. Automobiles have evolved from heavy works of iron and steel to an increasingly lighter architecture of high-strength plastic, aluminum, and other exotic materials.

Building upon the insights of Toynbee and Fuller, we can redefine progress by expanding the definition of ephemeralization. Progress can then be viewed as a two-fold process involving the simultaneous refinement of both the material and non-material side of life. With ephemeralization, the material side of life grows lighter, less burdensome, more articulate, and effortless. At the same time, the non-material side of life becomes more vital, expressive, knowledgeable, wise, artistic, and nurturing. In short, ephemeralization involves the co-evolution of inner and outer, consciousness and matter. Ephemeral progress does not negate the material side of life but calls forth a new partnership where the material and non-material aspects of life co-evolve with one another.

The outer aspects of our lives most important to ephemeralize are the basics: housing, transportation, food production, and energy generation. It is important to lighten up our inner aspects as well—learning the skills of touching the world and others ever more lightly and lovingly—in our relationships, work, community life, and more. With the combination of outer and inner refinement we have the potential for genuine progress, or building a sustainable *and* satisfying world for billions of people without devastating the ecology of the Earth. In place of a paradigm of consumerism we can embrace the more powerful, interesting and creative paradigm of *ephemeralism*.

We have seen that consumerism is a rational response if we view the universe as mostly dead matter and empty space. Consumerism offers us material pleasures, a sense of identity, and a measure of significance in an otherwise dead cosmos. In a non-living universe, it makes sense to exploit non-living matter on behalf of ourselves, because we are the most intensely alive creatures we know.

However, if we view the universe as fundamentally alive, a place perfectly suited for our awakening to that aliveness, then simplicity of living makes sense. Now we want to reduce the busyness and clutter that distract us from diving deep into existence. Seeing aliveness rather than deadness in the world around us, we feel less need for protection or even entertainment. We gather great satisfaction from the simple pleasures of engaging with others to share a conversation, a meal, or a walk. We see the significance of our lives in the size of our souls, not the size of our house, car, or bank account.

There are many names that we could give to this new approach to living: among them, voluntary simplicity, sophisticated simplicity, green living, ephemeral living, conserver living, and Earth-friendly living. Whatever we call this shift, it has dramatic implications for the future of our world.

At a global scale, to live sustainably we need to make much more efficient use of existing resources. To live more efficiently, it is vital to live more peacefully. Global military expenditures divert an enormous amount of human energy and material wealth that could otherwise be used for meeting basic human needs. To live more peacefully, it is essential to achieve a reasonable degree of fairness in material well-being. It is unrealistic to think that, in a communications-rich world, a large portion of the world's population will quietly accept living in absolute poverty and needless misery while a small minority lives in privileged comfort. Terrorism and civil unrest have their roots in desperate poverty and hopelessness. Without a revolution in fairness, the world seems destined to sink into endless conflict over scarce resources such as land, oil, and fresh water. In a self-fulfilling spiral of ruin, conflict over resources will increase demands for military expenditures and the potential for efficiency, equity, and long-term sustainability will diminish.

Instead of viewing simplicity as a lifestyle of limitation, it is important to recognize it as a path of global opportunity. Gandhi's principle of "live simply that others may simply live" is profoundly relevant. If the human family chooses a path of moderation and fairness, then hope will grow as billions of people assist one another in building a future of mutually assured development.

Earth-friendly, or green, ways of living are no longer alternative lifestyles for a pioneering few; instead, they are becoming conventional lifestyles for the mainstream majority, particularly in developed nations. Even with major technological innovations in energy and transportation, we will require dramatic changes in patterns of living and consuming if we are to maintain the integrity of the Earth as a living system. *Simplicity is simultaneously a personal choice, a civilizational choice, and a species choice.* We will make the choice for a sustainable future with much greater enthusiasm when we recognize that it is a necessary part of a future path that calls forth our species potentials and leads us into ever-greater communion with the living universe.

Creating New Kinds of Community

Our communion with the universe is mirrored in our expressions of community with one another. It is through community that we can most fully realize and celebrate ourselves as citizens of a sacred cosmos. Modern neighborhoods with isolated, single-family dwellings have been compared to tiny, underdeveloped nations where the potential for community and synergy has yet to be realized. A new architecture of life is required. In a shift similar to that which nature makes—for example, in the jump from simple atoms to complex molecules, or from complex molecules to living cells—humanity is being challenged to make a jump to a new level of community.

Because much of the urban infrastructure is already in place around the world, this means that a revolution in green retrofitting lies ahead as we reconfigure our lives to be sustainable in this new era. Rebuilding our cities and neighborhoods into islands of relative self-sufficiency—reducing dependency on distant sources of food, energy, and other material needs—will become the basis for a global economic revolution. A global "green village" movement is a healthy response to a world systems crisis because it will create a strong, resilient foundation for living.

Current patterns and scales of living do not suit emerging needs. The scale of the household is often too small, and a city too large, to realize many of the opportunities for sustainable living. Taking a lesson from humanity's past, I believe it is important to look at the in-between scale of living—that of a small village of a few hundred people. Whether newly built, or created by retrofitting an existing neighborhood or building, I believe great opportunity exists for the development of small, ecologically integrated villages ("eco-villages") to be nested within a larger urban area. I will use the term *eco-village* to describe the diverse expressions of new urban villages where the strength of one person or family meets the combined strength of others and, working together, something is created that was not possible before.

To illustrate from my own life, my partner Coleen and I have lived in an eco-village or co-housing community of about seventy people and we have seen how easily and quickly activities can be organized on that scale. From organizing fundraisers (such as a brunch for tsunami disaster relief), to arranging classes (from yoga to Cajun dancing), cultivating the garden, and creating community celebrations and events, we have participated in numerous gatherings that emerged with ease from the combined strengths and diverse talents of the community.

Looking ahead, I can imagine families in the future will live in an "eco-home" that is nested within an "eco-village," that is nested within an "eco-city," and so on up the scale to the bioregion, nation, and world. Each eco-village of several hundred people could have a distinct character, architecture, and economy. Most would likely contain: a childcare facility; a community house for meetings, celebrations, and meals; an organic community garden; a recycling and composting area; some revered open space; and a crafts/shop area. Each could offer their talents to support aspects of the local economy—the arts, healthcare, childcare, non-profit learning centers for gardening, green building, conflict resolution, and other skills—that would provide fulfilling employment for many. These micro-communities could have the culture and cohesiveness of a small town and the sophistication of a big city, as virtually everyone will be immersed within a world rich with communications. Eco-villages create the possibility for doing meaningful work, raising healthy children, celebrating life in community, and living in a way that seeks to honor the Earth and future generations. In looking at intentional communities emerging around the world, it is clear to me that a spiritual dimension is important in many of them. In turn, with the support of a conscious community, we can each grow into a more intimate relationship with the aliveness of the universe.

Because eco-villages, or co-housing communities, typically range in size from a hundred to several hundred people, they approximate the scale of a traditional tribe. Consequently, eco-villages are compatible with both the village-based cultures of indigenous societies and the needs of post-modern cultures. With a social and physical architecture sensitive to the psychology of modern tribes, a flowering of diverse communities—most created through retrofitting—could replace the alienation of today's massive cities. Diverse forms of eco-villages could provide the practical scale and foundation for a sustainable future. I believe new villages will become important islands of community, security, learning, and innovation in a world of sweeping change. These smaller-scale, human-sized living and working environments will foster diverse experiments in community and cooperative living. Overall, sustainability will be achieved through differing designs that are uniquely adapted to the culture, economy, interests, and environment of each locale.

Despite the appeal of eco-villages as a design for sustainable living, there is not the time to retrofit and rebuild our existing urban infrastructure before we hit an evolutionary wall. Climate disruption, energy shortages, and other critical trends will overtake us long before we have the opportunity to make a sweeping overhaul in the design and function of our cities and towns; therefore, it is important to learn from experiments in eco-villages and co-housing and to adapt their designs and principles for successful living to existing urban settings. Without the time to retrofit into well-designed green villages, we must make the most of the existing urban infrastructure and creatively adapt ourselves within it. Global challenges will produce a wave of green innovations for local living—technical, ecological, economic, social, architectural, and more. Lessons learned in eco-villages and co-housing will be important sources of invention and inspiration for a new village movement as existing urban architecture is transformed into human-scale designs for sustainable living.

Becoming Media-Conscious Citizens of the Earth

The mass media are a window through which we see the world. If the infusing aliveness of the universe is not recognized and celebrated in our media, then it is much less likely that we will see it in our everyday lives. If the media present diminished images of ourselves as isolated consumers who want to be entertained, then we will tend to fulfill that self-image. However, if we see portrayals of ourselves as citizens of the cosmos who are actively engaged in a heroic journey of awakening, we will tend to fulfill that self-image. Because the mass media are so powerful in presenting and reinforcing our self-image as a species, it is critical that we use this storytelling machine of mass culture to tell ourselves bigger stories about where we are, who we are, and where we are going.

Learning to see ourselves in the collective mirror of the mass media is as important as learning to see ourselves in the mirror of our personal consciousness. Once there is inclusive and sustained social reflection, we can build a working consensus regarding appropriate actions for a promising future. We are a visual species; we cannot consciously build a positive future that we have not first *collectively* imagined. When we can see a sustainable and promising future, we can build it. Actions can then come quickly and voluntarily. Voluntary or self-organized action will be vital to success because hundreds of millions of people will be required to act in cooperation with one another. With local to global communication, we can mobilize ourselves purposefully, and each can contribute their unique talents to the creation of a life-affirming future.

At the very time that humanity requires a dramatic new level of human communications, the converging media of television and the Internet are making the world transparent to itself. Our world is bursting with conversation from the grassroots, and bringing an entirely new layer of conversation and connection into global culture. We now can see climate disruption producing crop failures and famine in Africa, destruction of rain forests in Brazil, coastlines eroding from hurricanes in the United States, violent conflict fueled by religious differences in the Middle East, and the impact of skyrocketing energy prices around the world. Television and the Internet make every person a global witness—a knowing and feeling participant in world affairs. We have access to a world of vastly greater diversity and depth than ever before.

There is a weakness in the very strength of the Internet. The vast outpouring of views and voices from the grassroots is flooding us with a confusing avalanche of messages. Without a way to discover a working consensus, we are paralyzed. To coalesce our collective sentiments, we require regular opportunities for millions, and even billions, of persons to gather and explore our common future. We have all the technology needed to hold interactive electronic town meetings (via television and the Internet) that dramatically advance the conversation of democracy and provide us with a powerful voice in choosing our future. We need only the social will to claim that potential.

The scope and quality of our collective attention is the most precious resource we have as a human community. If we don't pay attention while decisions of monumental importance are being made, then we effectively forfeit our future. The bottom line is this: If we are to take practical steps to awaken our society, then citizens must make their voices heard in creating a more reflective and responsive media environment. I recognize many people feel profoundly disempowered when it comes to media change. Nonetheless, it is essential to leave that disempowerment in the past. The media are the most visible representation of our collective mind. As the media goes, so goes the future. Currently, our collective mind is being programmed for commercial success and evolutionary failure.

Building a culture of sustainability will require as much creativity, energy, and enthusiasm as we have invested in building cultures of consumption. It is vital we begin conversations about sustainability at a scale that matches the actual scope of the challenges we face—and often these are of regional, national, and global scale. The world has become intensely interdependent. Our consciousness and conversations need to match the scale of the world in which we live. This is a time for rapid learning and experimentation locally, all the while being mindful of how we connect globally.

At this pivotal moment in our history, a citizen's movement for a more conscious democracy could turn humanity's primary attention machine—television—from the distractions of adolescent entertainment towards a mature reflection on matters of momentous concern. As the world's systems problems converge into the singularity of a global systems crisis, we could pause in our normal affairs and finally tell ourselves the truth. The business-as-usual focus of global media on commerce and entertainment could be replaced by a critical period of planetary truth telling in which we humans work to heal the wounds of history and then, together, forge a vision of a sustainable and meaningful future.

It was communication that enabled humans to evolve from early hunter-gatherers to the verge of planetary civilization, and it will be communication that enables us to become a bonded human family committed to the well-being of all. At the very time that we need an unprecedented capacity for local-to-global communication, we find we have the necessary tools in abundance. Electronic gatherings will blossom from the local to national to global scale and make the sentiments of the body politic highly visible. When everyone knows the "whole world is watching"—when economic, ethnic, ideological, and religious violence is brought before the court of world public opinion through the Internet and the other media—it will bring a powerful corrective influence into human relations. As groups and nations see their actions scrutinized and judged by the rest of the world community, we will become more inclined to search for ethical and nonviolent approaches.

Because communication is fundamental to our common future, it is critical that the human community work consciously to bridge the digital divide, extend the communications culture to all corners of the globe, and build an effective "social mirror" for the human family—one that authentically reflects both the adversities and the opportunities of our times. All cultures will be naked—their history forever exposed in a world made transparent by the electronic media—and confronted with the need to make amends for wrongs committed in the past if there is to be release into a promising future. A supreme challenge will be to hold a steady and undistorted social mirror as we struggle for collective understanding, respect, and reconciliation. Societies without a tradition of freedom of speech will find this both liberating and extremely demanding as new skills of inclusion and reconciliation are required to participate effectively.

One of the most helpful and powerful actions we can take as we move through this transition as a species is to increase opportunities for conscious reflection from the personal to the planetary scale. Personal reflection refers to seeing ourselves in the mirror of consciousness as individuals and to observe the unfolding of our lives. By analogy, social reflection refers to seeing ourselves in the mirror of collective consciousness by using tools such as the mass media.

The more widely and accurately our time of initiation is witnessed by the people of the Earth through the global media, the more strongly the lessons of this time will be grounded in our collective lives and memory; in turn, the less likely it is that we will have to relearn these lessons in the future. If we can see disasters in our social imagination, we may not need to manifest them in our actual experience. As societies, we can collectively imagine futures that we do not want to enact in experience—futures marked by profound climate change, resource shortages, famine, and conflict. If we use our collective imagination to see that perpetuating the status quo produces a future that few would want, then we can consciously turn in a more promising direction.

With social reflection from the local to global scale, we can explore the core questions raised here: Is the universe dead or alive? Who are we as a species? What kind of journey are we on? As our capacity for social reflection grows, we can choose social conversations more wisely and look for promising pathways more effectively. Actions can come quickly and voluntarily as we develop a capacity for building consensus for a promising future. With a shared vision, each person can contribute unique talents in creating that future. Voluntary, self-organizing action will be vital to our success. Our swiftly developing world situation is far too complex for any one individual, group, or nation to design remedies that will work for everyone. While being mindful of the conditions and needs at the global scale, we can work creatively at the local scale to adapt to changing conditions. This is a time for diverse local experimentation undertaken in a context of rich communication from the local to the global levels.

Bringing Our True Gifts into the World

At this time of supreme testing, we are being challenged to give nothing less than our highest and best gifts to the world. The Buddhist monk Thich Nhat Hanh describes how we each have what can be called "near gifts" and "true gifts." Near gifts, he says, are those things that we are pretty good at doing. Often we make our living and have our lives absorbed in our near gifts. He also said that we each have true gifts. True gifts are those things in which we are soulfully gifted—activities in which we feel at ease, where we naturally excel, and that bring us happiness in our personal lives and the lives of others. I believe the times ahead will be so demanding that our near gifts will not be sufficient to get us through. At this rare moment in history when our human capacities are being tested to their utmost, we are each challenged to bring our true gifts into the world. The window of opportunity is brief. Don't hold back. Give your gifts to the world at this pivotal moment in the human journey.

The Promise of the Journey Ahead

We have come full circle in the great story of our journey of return to our cosmic home. Now we can look again at the three questions that have oriented this inquiry.

Where are we? The combined wisdom of science and spirituality speak with stunning clarity. We live, not in a dead universe, but in a living universe that is almost entirely invisible, flowing with an immensity of energy, continuously emerging anew, and brimming with sentience. We live in a universe that is vastly larger, more alive, subtle, intelligent, purposeful, and free than many of us have begun to imagine. With humility, we can turn back to the cosmos and freshly rediscover our home.

Who are we? Life exists within life. Our life is inseparable from the aliveness of the living universe. Our aliveness and consciousness extends beyond our biological bodies and into the further reaches and depths of the living universe. Our physical bodies comprise only the smallest fraction of the full scope of our being. Our bodies are biodegradable vehicles for learning that we are subtle beings of light, love, music, and knowing. We may have thought we were physical beings in a material universe, but now we are discovering that we are beings who are an integral part of the life stream of a living universe. With renewed feelings of wonder, we can open to a larger sense of self that connects into the subtle aliveness of a living universe.

Where are we going? Humanity is growing up and growing into the reality that we are beings of both biological and cosmic dimension. We are on a heroic journey of awakening — learning how to live within the deep ecology of the Mother Universe. Our journey of awakening and discovery has reached a critical stage. We now confront the supreme test of living sustainably on the Earth, in harmony with one another, and in communion with the living universe. If we can make the great turn toward home — if we can move from a path of separation to a path of communion and connection with our home, the universe, then humanity's journey can continue to unfold. We can move into an era of reflection and reconciliation as a human family, then beyond into an era of deep bonding and restoration, and then into an era of flowing creativity. We have far to go and much to learn to complete our magnificent journey of awakening.

We live in momentous times and the choices we make now will powerfully influence the future course of evolution on the Earth. In these historic times, a paramount task for the human community is to discover a larger sense of identity and vision for the human journey, one that can bring us together in a common enterprise. The doorway into a larger understanding of who we are and where we are going can be found by becoming more conscious of where we already are—living within a living universe. In discovering we live within a living universe, we open to the heartening knowledge we are one of her precious offspring, seeking communion with her depths. We celebrate that the living universe has a central project—growing self-referencing streams of life at every scale—and that we are one flowering of an evolutionary dynamic at work throughout the cosmos. In seeing the universe around us as alive, we consciously seek to grow that aliveness within ourselves. What a wonderful paradox: We get our bearings for the journey ahead by recognizing that we are already home.

Chapter 9

Living in a Living Universe

Reading about the living universe and what it means for our lives offers one level of learning. A deeper and more powerful level of learning unfolds when we bring these insights into our lives through direct experience and shared conversations. To suggest a few possibilities, I've drawn themes from the book and placed them in two sections—meditations and dialogues. I encourage you to explore and expand upon these as a way to deepen your engagement with our living universe. For additional resources, see my website at www.awakeningearth.org.

Meditations

Ultimately, the goal of meditation is simply to relax into "ordinary reality" which, as we have seen, is quite extraordinary. Because the universe is alive, when we slow down, calm down, and come into the moment, we are opening into a subtle field of conscious aliveness. Instead of striving to reach some imagined state of awakening, in meditation we relax the thinking mind, rest in the simplicity of the moment, and allow the miracle of a living universe to present itself in our direct experience. We don't have to *do* anything. We are only required to be open in our experience — to be curious and awake to everyday life — and the first miracle of a living universe will become self-evident in our awareness. In that spirit, here are a few meditations drawn from this book that can support our awakening to a living universe.

Imagine Building a Universe (see Chapter 1)

Find a space without distraction and reread this section. In your imagination, feel yourself meeting the challenge of these building requirements. This exercise is not about understanding physics, it is about amazement and wordless understanding. Without words, feel the questions: What kind of universe is this? What kind of reality are we living within? What am I? Can I notice creation happening? As you go through the day, notice that the universe is *not* static but instead is a dynamic, evolving entity that is being continuously regenerated at every moment — and you are one of its manifestations that can know this because you have a capacity for reflective consciousness.

Seeing Ourselves as Giants (see Chapter 1)

Take the time to clearly visualize the cosmic ruler that runs from the largest to the smallest scale in the known universe. Take time to get a direct, bodily feeling for the largest scale with its millions of galaxies. When the immensity of the universe beyond us is felt, then turn your attention inward to recognize that an even greater immensity lies within. Feeling ourselves between these immensities, we see that our true size (relative to the scale of the universe) is vastly bigger than we thought. Regularly notice yourself as a giant. Experience that we have more smallness within ourselves than there is bigness beyond ourselves.[1] Appreciate that, without close attention, we could overlook much that is happening in the realm of the very small.

Opening to Our Invisible Self (see Chapter 1)

The known universe is almost entirely invisible and is comprised of two unseen forces—one pushing the universe outward in expansion and another pulling the universe inward in contraction. If the overwhelming majority of the universe is invisible, then how much of ourselves is invisible as well? If we participate in an ecology of consciousness, how far does our aliveness reach? We are giants in the material scale of things and we are colossal when we include the non-material scope of our being. When we relax into our direct experience, we are opening into a field of aliveness that is boundless. Every situation provides an opportunity to explore this invisible aspect of life and to make friends with your "self" as both a biological and cosmological being.

Looking into Space (see Chapter 2)

We tend to take space for granted and focus on the material objects in life. Instead of looking *through* space, we can look *into* space and see the aliveness of the universe. Space is not a pre-existing emptiness but a dynamically constructed transparency. Space is filled with energy, activity, and geometry. The fabric of space-time is being continuously created anew. Look for the subtle, dancing aliveness of that process. With soft eyes and a relaxed awareness, open to the energy and dynamism that shimmers within the fabric of living space. This is a wonderful meditation to practice when you can sit quietly, look out into an open space and receive its presence.

Cultivating Reflective Consciousness (see Chapter 7)

The first step in awakening is to develop our capacity for paying attention to ourselves as we move through life. Instead of running on automatic, we can gently notice ourselves in the mirror of consciousness as we go through the world. We can cultivate a witnessing consciousness as we move through the day. From our bodily sensations and emotional responses to our ever-changing thoughts—all are suitable for reflection in the mirror of consciousness. Without any need for change, our only task is simply to observe ourselves moving through life. This requires that we make friends with ourselves and become comfortable with our self-presence. In this process we are also making friends with, and relaxing into, the living universe. Each spiritual tradition has its unique vehicle for awakening to life by cultivating a reflective consciousness; among these are meditation, contemplation, prayer, chanting, yoga, and more. It is important to discover the approach that fits your life and to make a commitment to cultivating a reflective consciousness.

Opening to Oceanic Consciousness (see Chapter 7)

We all exist within the same ocean of aliveness and, with heartfelt attention and openness, we can become permeable to the subtle presence of this larger ecology of life. As the polarity of "knower and known" merge into a unified awareness, we enter the infusing ecology of conscious aliveness that is the living universe. A precise and calm attention is required to sustain this centered experience of subtle communion. In experiencing ourselves as part of a much larger field of life, the well-being of all life becomes a compelling concern. A powerful meditation is to practice opening to the direct experience of the field of life. It is to be awake without judgment and from a place of stillness and centeredness. Include all faculties for wordless sensing and knowing. Celebrate glimpses. Communion is priceless.

Practicing Flow Consciousness and Reality Surfing (see Chapter 7)

As we become familiar with the subtle ocean of aliveness, we find that it is not still but forever flowing into existence. In letting go of the witnessing self, we experience reality surfing as we ride the wave of the ever-arising universe. When our movement through life as free beings is in harmony with the flow of the arising universe, then there is a feeling of being with the flow. Although this description is simple, the practice is exquisitely difficult and requires the highest levels of concentration and relaxation. A starting point is the practice of mindfulness and learning to live in the present moment. With mindfulness, everything we do provides an occasion for an observing consciousness: driving, walking, playing, eating, or washing the dishes. Flow consciousness is no different, except that it elevates attention to a much higher level of precision, openness, and continuity, enabling us to ride the regenerative wave of the ever-arising universe.

Recognizing Ourselves Before We Die (see Chapter 5)

Our responsibility is to use this life to recognize and develop ourselves as a body of light, love, music, and knowing. Light is a fundamental building block of the universe; we are literally beings of light. Rather than take qualities and textures of light for granted, we can notice and taste these differences in our awareness. Try sitting with soft eyes and relaxed attention, receiving the presence of the surrounding light.

We are also a body of resonance, or music. All that exists is vibrating with its unique resonance. We can listen for the hum of existence. In meeting another person, we can listen for the unique song of their soul. In each new situation, we can open to the feeling-tones and qualities of resonance people express. We can discover subtle feelings of harmony or disharmony and express our unique songline as we move through life.

The aliveness at the foundation of the universe has a distinct quality that has been called love. We can cultivate our awareness of the feeling tone of life.

Finally, each person embodies a distinctive orchestration of knowing that reflects our unique life experience. That knowing is not confined to our physical body; it also infuses the ecology of the universe and the atmosphere of existence. A core practice is to nurture a body of knowing that feels whole and congruent.

I often pay attention to one of these four qualities of the soul as I go through the day, and then spontaneously select a moment to ask myself, "If I were to die at this very moment, would I recognize myself?" I look for a wordless answer to the question, recognizing that death is an ally for awakening to my most authentic self.

Conversations

Another important way to bring the living universe into your life is in conversation with others. The idea of a living universe generates seeds for many conversations. With a spirit of open inquiry, where there are no right or wrong answers, discussions can move into interesting and unexpected areas. To keep the conversation alive, it is vital to have a balance of voices and the curiosity to discover other points of view. The purpose of these conversations is not to persuade but to understand one another and ourselves more fully.

I encourage you to dive into these conversations—in your home, at school, at work, in your blogs, and on the web. Consider inviting friends and associates to explore these questions in a conversation circle. For support of conversation circles go to my website (www.awakeningearth.org), where you can find writings on diverse topics, streaming videos, key links, online courses, and more. Here are a few of my favorite conversations on the theme of a living universe.

Is the Universe Dead or Alive at its Foundations?

This is a powerful question. Be prepared for strong points of view; people often have an immediate response. Some people view the universe as non-living at the foundations, see space as empty, matter as inert, and believe that we as living creatures have evolved from empty space and inert matter. "It is nothing more than fantasy and superstition to think the whole universe is alive." Other people respond instantly, saying "Of course it's alive, how could you think otherwise? It is incomprehensible that the experiences of awe evoked by the universe could arise unless the world around us is alive." This book provides ample information with which to begin a dialogue that includes both science and spirituality.

What Difference Does It Make? (see Introduction)

How will our lives be different with one perspective versus another? What difference does it make if we think the universe is unconscious and indifferent to humanity or else aware and non-interfering? Would we act differently if we knew that our actions and intentions were forever woven into the invisible ecology of a living universe? Would we look at our personal lives and time on this Earth differently if we were to regard the universe as a living and learning system that supports our awakening, in freedom, to ever greater aliveness and creative participation?

What Is the Life Stage of Humanity? (see Chapters 7 and 8)

This is a great question to explore.[2] (See my website for a short video, ongoing survey, and writing on this theme.) There are no right answers, but there is often a very high level of agreement that surprises everyone. I begin by asking people to discuss the life stage of our species as reflected in our collective behavior. After five to ten minutes, I ask them to come up with a "social average" and choose among these four stages for the species: toddler, teenager, adult, and elder. An overwhelming majority of the groups vote that humanity is in its adolescence. Interestingly, the reasons given are much the same around the world. Then I ask them to consider a second question: What was most important for you in making the journey from adolescence to adulthood? — the premise being that what was important for you at a personal level is probably going to be relevant to the human family at a global level. This conversation reveals that, as important as, for example, a new energy policy may be for humanity's future, even more important are efforts to awaken a new level of collective maturity that includes a more conscious relationship with the living universe.

Where Are We on the Hero's Journey? (see Chapter 7)

Instead of viewing ourselves as villains who are destroying the Earth, can we see ourselves as evolutionary heroes? Can we regard ourselves as a pioneering species that is on an epic journey of awakening? Around the world, people understand the hero's journey; it is a classic journey with three major stages: separation, initiation, and return. A powerful conversation can emerge by asking people where they think we are as a human community relative to these three stages. Are we still separating from nature? Are we encountering a supreme test and a time of species initiation? Have we already turned the corner and begun a journey of return?

Are We an Observing Species? (see Chapters 7 and 8)

How fully are we living up to our species name? Our name expresses our potential: we are *Homo sapien sapiens,* the beings who "know that we know." We have the ability to reflect upon ourselves, to see ourselves in the mirror of our own consciousness. How well are we using our tools of collective observation and reflection—the mass media—to assist in responding to the many challenges of our times? To what extent are the media awakening us to the world and to what extent are they distracting and deadening us? If there were a great emergency and threat to the Earth, could we collectively "wake up" and have a shared conversation as a species? If you had a minute or two of air time on global television, what story or vision for our species would you want to tell?

Are We a Cosmic Species? (see Chapter 8)

At the heart of this book is the insight that we are not separate from the flow of the ever-arising universe. This reality is so subtle that it is difficult to discern or describe. However, as we develop a literacy of consciousness and the ability to pay attention, we can experience firsthand our participation in the subtle field of aliveness and our connection with the ecology of the universe. In turn, we recognize that we are beings of both biological and cosmic dimension. Do you think of yourself as a being of both biological and cosmological nature and scope? In what ways?

Imagining Scenarios for the Future? (see Chapter 8)

Combining the four preceding archetypes in different ways, we can construct scenarios from promising to ruinous. As the culmination of a series of conversations, you could ask a conversation circle to integrate these four archetypes into coherent scenarios or stories about how the world will unfold in the coming generation. Are we growing up? Moving through our time of initiation? Becoming more reflective as a species? Recognizing we are participants in cosmic scale evolution? What does "progress" look like with different combinations of archetypes? How important is high-consumption materialism to visions of progress?

How Can Simplicity Support Engaging Aliveness? (see Chapter 8)

Many questions can reveal the value of simplicity in a living universe. Assuming we are immersed within a living universe, how can I bring more of this subtle miracle into my everyday life? How can I reduce the unnecessary busyness, clutter, and complexity that distract me from this ever-present miracle? How can I live with greater balance between inner and outer aspects of my life? How can the core areas of my life—home, diet, work, transportation—reflect my concern and respect for the larger ecology of life? How can I live undivided and whole in my relationship between my work and humanity's future?

What Are Your Near Gifts and True Gifts? (see Chapter 8)

We face enormous challenges and will have to re-invent the world in which we live—including where and how we work, community life and structure, education, food systems, transportation, and more. Now is not the time for half-hearted contributions—the world needs our greatest talents. What are your greatest gifts? We all have "near gifts," or things that we are pretty good at doing. In addition, we each have "true gifts" that express our unique talents, interests, and abilities. What are your true gifts? In what ways could your true gifts be in service of humanity's future?

With reflection, vision, conversation, and action, we can make the journey into a promising future. An extraordinary journey beckons us. What more could we ask for? The universe is a learning system and we are students of eternity. We are only halfway home. Let's get on with the adventure—learning to live in our living universe.

Notes

Preface

1. The "Warning to Humanity" was sponsored by the Union of Concerned Scientists, 26 Church St., Cambridge, MA 02238.

Introduction

1. Thomas Berry, *Riverdale Papers VII*, "The American College in the Ecological Age," Riverdale Center, 1980.
2. Susan Blackmore, see: "Zen Meditation Leaves Consciousness Scientist Skeptical," *Skeptiko*, March 5, 2007. See: http://www.skeptiko.com/index.php?id=12.
3. It is important not to equate the idea of a dead universe with atheism. Most atheists focus on denying the existence of an external deity, saying this idea is beyond the reach of scientific investigation. The living universe hypothesis is not focused on an external deity but on the here and now. Whether the universe is living or non-living is a subject for scientific inquiry. This means that someone could be an atheist (not believe in an external deity) and at the same time regard the universe as profoundly alive. Conversely, someone could be a theist (believe in an external deity) and at the same time regard the universe around us as non-living. It seems more likely that someone would be a theist and view the universe as living. However, no particular religious orientation automatically fits persons who regard the universe as alive.

Chapter 1

1. Walt Whitman, "Song of the Open Road," from *Leaves of Grass*, 1900.
2. Bill Broder, *The Sacred Hoop*, San Francisco: Sierra Club Books, 1979.

3. The Planck length is the unit of length approximately 1.6×10^{-35} meters, or about 10^{-20} times the diameter of a proton. The Planck length is deemed "natural" because it can be defined from three fundamental physical constants: the speed of light, Planck's constant, and the gravitational constant.

4. Joel Primack and Nancy Abrams, *The View from the Center of the Universe*, New York: Riverhead Books, 2006. Also, see their website: http://viewfromthecenter.com/index.html.

5. Primack and Abrams, ibid., p. 174.

6. About 4% of the total energy density in the universe (as inferred from gravitational effects) can be seen directly. About 23% is thought to be composed of dark matter, and the remaining 73% is thought to consist of dark energy. See, for example, David Cline, "The Search for Dark Matter," in *Scientific American*, February 2003.

7. In physical cosmology, dark energy is an exotic form of energy that permeates all of space and tends to increase the rate of expansion of the universe. See, for example, P. J. E. Peebles and Bharat Ratra (2003), "The cosmological constant and dark energy," *Reviews of Modern Physics* 75: 559–606. doi:10.1103/RevModPhys.75.559.

8. See the overview by Robert Lawrence Kuhn, "Why This Universe? Toward a Taxonomy of Possible Explanations," in *Skeptic*, Volume 13, Number 2, 2007. Also, Alex Villenkin, *Many Worlds in One: The Search for Other Universes*, New York: Hill & Wang, 2006.

9. See: Dean Radin, *The Conscious Universe,* San Francisco: Harper Edge, 1997. Also see Dean Radin, *Entangled Minds: Extrasensory Experiences in a Quantum Reality*, New York: Paraview Pocket Books, 2006.

10. Dean Radin, *The Conscious Universe* (1997) and *Entangled Minds* (2006), op. cit.

11. See: Andrew Greeley and William McCready, "Are We a Nation of Mystics," in *The New York Times Magazine*, January 26, 1975. [Elsewhere Greeley states that "...as much as one-fifth of the population has frequent mystical experiences." See: Andrew Greeley, *Ecstasy as a Way of Knowing*, Englewood Cliffs, NJ: Prentice-Hall, 1974, p. 57.] Also reported in *Brain/Mind Bulletin* 12:7 (March, 1987), p. 1; and Andrew Greeley, "The Impossible: It's Happening," *Noetic Sciences Review*, Sausalito, California, Spring, 1987, pp. 7–9. A regional poll conducted in the San Francisco Bay Area gives more conservative, but still striking, results. It found that

27% said they had experienced being "very close to a powerful spiritual force that seemed to lift people out of themselves." Reported in *San Francisco Chronicle*, Tuesday, April 24, 1990. A survey conducted by the National Opinion Research Center at the University of Chicago asked a sampling of persons in the United States whether they had ever had experiences that could be interpreted as "mystical." They discovered that among the random sample, 55% said they had experienced "a feeling of deep and profound peace," 43% said they felt "love is at the center of everything," 29% described an experience "of the unity of everything and my own part in it," and 25% had the "sense that all the universe is alive." This poll indicates that the experience of intimate union with all of creation is far more widespread than commonly acknowledged.

12. It is important to clarify the two different meanings that are given to the phrase *intelligent design*. I refer often, in various ways, to the intelligent design that is expressed so clearly and beautifully throughout nature and the universe. However, an appreciation of the intelligent design of the universe should not be equated with the theological view of the same name. Specifically, many Christian fundamentalists believe that "intelligent design" offers an alternative explanation to biological evolution. In this view, an outside force created, all at the same time, the diversity in plants and animals that we see in the world today without the need for any evolution; therefore, the exquisite design of the universe is not a result of 14 billion years of unfolding in freedom but rather has been externally directed and created all at once by an external deity. The view I present regards the universe as a living system that is being continuously regenerated and that has been designed to support, in freedom, the evolutionary development of self-referencing and self-organizing systems at every scale. Instead of a deterministic universe, freedom is built into the quantum foundations of the universe. Nonetheless, because the universe is a whole system where everything interacts with and depends upon everything else, freedom has limits. Within the constraints of the universe as an integrated, interdependent system, we can act and create in freedom. Because our level of freedom grows as we become more conscious (of where we are, who we are, and the journey we are on), it means that our freedom is increasing as we awaken. Instead of being the product of an external designer, our universe appears to be an "inside job"—we are all co-creative participants in this learning and evolving system.

13. See: Duane Elgin, *Awakening Earth,* New York: Morrow, 1993, pp. 304–5.

Chapter 2

1. Albert Einstein, Banesh Hoffman, and Helen Dukas, *Albert Einstein, The Human Side*, Princeton University Press, 1979.

2. See: John Roach, "Alien Life May Be 'Weirder' Than Scientists Think," *National Geographic News,* July 6, 2007. The article describes the report by the National Academy of Sciences on the search for extraterrestrial life. Also see: "From plasma crystals and helical structures towards inorganic living matter," V. N. Tsytovich et al., 2007, *New J Phys* 9:263. http://www.iop.org/EJ/abstract/1367-2630/9/8/263.

3. Lee Smolin, *The Life of the Cosmos*, New York: Oxford University Press, 1997, pp. 252–53.

4. David Bohm, *Wholeness and the Implicate Order*, London: Routledge and Kegan Paul, 1980, p. 175.

5. Michael Talbot, *The Holographic Universe*, New York: HarperCollins, 1991.

6. John Wheeler, quoted in Fritjof Capra, *The Tao of Physics*, Boulder, CO: Shambhala, 1975, p. 128.

7. Sir James Jeans, *The Mysterious Universe*, London: Cambridge University Press, 1931, p. 121.

8. Ibid., p. 191.

9. See, for example: http://freeenergynews.com/Directory/ZPE/index.html.

10. David Bohm, op. cit., pp.190–91.

11. Sir James Jeans, op. cit., p. 259.

12. For a further discussion, see my article, "The Living Cosmos: A Theory of Continuous Creation," *ReVision*, Summer 1988. Also see my book *Awakening Earth*, Chapter 11, "Continuous Creation of the Cosmos." A fundamental theme throughout this book is that the universe is continually arising anew at each moment. In turn, this raises the question: At what speed is the cosmos coming into existence? The speed of emergence, or the pace of arising of the overall cosmic system, cannot be determined objectively because we cannot stand outside the cosmos in its process of becoming itself and measure it coming into existence. Because we are inside and integral to this flow of continuous regeneration, we can only make inferences regarding the pace at which this flow is occurring. For insight, we turn to a fundamental attribute of the cosmos—the constancy of the speed of light. Continuous creation cosmology hypothesizes that the *constancy* of the speed of light is a result of the precise *consistency* with which the overall fabric of

the universe is dynamically woven together. In other words, the constancy of the speed of light is produced by, and is a result of, the pervasive evenness with which the overall cosmos is being regenerated as a unified system. In turn, the precise consistency of continuous creation at the cosmic scale has been interpreted as the constancy of the speed of light at the local scale.

Continuous-creation theory suggests a straightforward reason for the physical compression, time dilation, and increase in mass predicted by relativity theory as an object approaches the speed of light. Assuming the overall cosmos is being woven together in a continuous flow whose pace is revealed by the constancy of the speed of light, then when an "object" (as a flow-through, standing wave) approaches the speed of light it will necessarily run into itself in the process of becoming itself, and this will produce a literal compression of its dynamic structure in its direction of motion. No thing (as a standing wave) can move ahead of the flow that continuously regenerates both the object and the surrounding cosmos. As an object (flow-through subsystem of the larger standing-wave cosmos) tries to move ahead of the pace at which it is becoming manifest, it will progressively run into itself becoming itself—a self-limiting process that produces the increasing physical compression, time dilation, and mass predicted by relativity theory. Assuming our cosmos is a flow-through system that is being continuously regenerated at each moment, then this should logically produce a limiting condition (boundary, threshold) as any object approaches the rate of regeneration for the overall system. No object within the dynamically arising system can move ahead of (or outside of) the system within which and from which it is continuously arising and coming into manifest existence.

A "cosmic now" is assumed to embrace all the workings of the fifth dimension and beyond, even while each object is assumed to retain a unique time status in the lesser dimensions. Our cosmos is continuously recreated with millions of years of time-delay or relativistic lag-time built into its fourth-dimensional aspect (for example, the time it takes a signal to travel from the Andromeda galaxy to our own), while simultaneously being completely up-to-date in its fifth-dimensional aspect. While relativity theory rightly dismissed simultaneity in four dimensions, continuous creation cosmology reintroduces simultaneity as a basic property of the fifth dimension and beyond. Simultaneity serves a vital purpose—to instantaneously distribute operating information regarding the status of sub-systems to all parts of the cosmos and thereby keep the dynamic structure of the universe in equilibrium with itself. With simultaneity in the fifth and higher dimensions, no interval is required to factor changes into the flow of manifestation of the overall cosmos. Each object has its unique four-dimensional existence and, at the same time, all objects share equally in the flow of continuous creation. Therefore, irrespective of relativistic differences (separation in time and space), all things throughout the cosmos share equally in the flow of continuous creation. The NOW of holo-dynamic, five-dimensional manifestation is the same for all entities, and all places, throughout the cosmos. Relativistic time in four dimensions is stretchy and varies for each object, while the time of the fifth dimension is absolute and unvarying for all objects. Time flows within the relativistic framework of four dimensions and dissolves into holographic simultaneity in five dimensions and beyond.

To visualize the dynamic of continuous creation, imagine that the universe is a unified hologram that is being projected into existence at each moment with all relativistic differences fully coordinated out of a context of five dimensions or more. Also imagine that a spacecraft inside this giant hologram is being beamed into existence along with everything else as a continuous flow of manifestation. Then imagine that the spacecraft begins to move ahead at an increasing speed so that it approaches the speed with which the hologram-universe is being projected into existence. Since the craft is a projection as well, it cannot move outside of the hologram of which it is an integral part because if it tries to do so it will increasingly run into itself becoming itself, producing the seemingly impossible conditions at the extremes of relativity theory (becoming shorter in the direction of motion, increasing mass, and relativistic time slowing down). To reiterate, I assume that the constancy of the speed of light at the local scale is a result of a larger process occurring at the cosmic scale—the precise consistency of manifestation of our entire cosmos as a single, standing wave embracing both the fabric of space-time and matter-energy.

This theory of a regenerating cosmos suggests why the mass of an object increases as it accelerates toward light speed. As the object approaches light speed, it will have to draw ever greater increments of energy from the larger ecological system as it attempts to move ahead of the ecological processes that dynamically create it. Increasing energy is required to approach light speed because, in reality, the object is trying to overcome itself in the process of becoming itself—a self-limiting process that requires drawing ever greater increments of energy from the larger cosmological system. As the object draws down ever-greater increments of energy to maintain its dynamic structure, mass must also increase, given the convertibility of matter and energy.

With regard to slowing relativistic time, as an object approaches light speed it runs into itself in the process of its own becoming and compresses what otherwise would have been realized actuality back into the domain of unrealized potential. The process seems analogous to walking against the direction of motion on a moving conveyer belt, or walking up an escalator as it moves down. By walking against the direction of movement, dynamic stasis is approached. Similarly, as an object approaches light speed, it increasingly runs into its dynamically generated structure, thereby compressing itself relative to the rest of the freely manifesting cosmos—one measured result being a slowing of relativistic time. If the object were to reach light speed, then it would be running into itself as fast as it manifests, and this would effectively cancel out its process of becoming relative to the rest of the four-dimensional flow—thereby effectively stopping relativistic time.

Ernst Mach attributed inertia (resistance to motion) to an object's interaction with the totality of matter throughout the universe. However, Mach's theory presents a major difficulty: An unknown force must act instantaneously among all material objects throughout the cosmos and yet, within the confines of a four-dimensional cosmology, it is impossible for forces to act instantaneously. The continuous creation model provides a source for instantaneous connection—it assumes each object is a dynamically generated resonance pattern that is always connected with the entire cosmos at each instant. Inertia results when an "object" presses against the "cosmos"—a giant, unified resonance pattern. If an object moves outside the natural flow of the surrounding cosmos, it will push against the flow of the cosmos becoming itself, and this will be experienced as resistance to motion, or inertia. Inertia is a measure of the energy required to change the motion of an object relative to the natural momentum of the entire fabric of the dynamically manifesting cosmos. To accomplish a path change anywhere requires an instantaneous and compensating change everywhere.

As to coordinating the interweaving of an entire universe, it is helpful to consider Planck's constant, which may be a conversion factor for continuous creation. No matter what energy level a photon of light may have, it must be packaged (as a quanta) in such a way that its combined energy and wavelength are exactly equal to the universal constant h, or Planck's constant. A shorter wavelength is accompanied by higher frequencies and higher energies, and vice versa. Assuming four-dimensional reality is generated at light speed, Planck's constant could represent the conversion factor for keeping all differences in motion, mass, and energy in precise orchestration with one another—thereby preserving the unbroken fabric of four-dimensional reality. Differences in the frequency, wavelength, and energy of light (as it coalesces from the fifth-plus dimensions and into the fourth), could be used to produce the diverse material world we inhabit. Planck's constant seems to be the conversion factor for precisely governing the flow of light as it enters into four-dimensional reality and visible manifestation.

This cosmology may also be useful in resolving the dilemma of the arrow of time. Stated differently, a key conceptual problem with faster-than-light signaling is that it can generate time paradoxes. If a signal is able to reach into the past or future, then time order and causality are impossible to establish, and the result is immense confusion. Continuous creation cosmology resolves this dilemma by postulating that, while events can have a space-like separation in four dimensions, they have fully instantaneous connection in the fifth and higher dimensions. Because the entire four-dimensional cosmos is created whole at each instant, the flow of manifestation includes all lags and differentials in relativistic time. Due to full simultaneity, there is no time-forward or time-reversed signaling in the higher dimensions. There can be no "stand back" signaling because all times are complete at each instant.

Because the continuous creation hypothesis offers a wide range of insights, it seems to be a valuable addition to theories regarding the nature and evolution of the universe.

13. Guy Murchie, *Music of the Spheres*, Cambridge, Massachusetts: The Riverside Press, 1961, p. 451.

14. Max Born, *The Restless Universe*, New York: Harper & Brothers, 1936, p. 277.

15. Albert Einstein, "The Concept of Space," *Nature*, 125, 1930, pp. 897–98.

16. Walter Moore, *Schrodinger: Life and Thought*, New York: Cambridge University Press, 1989.

17. Bohm, op. cit., p. 11.

18. Norbert Wiener, *The Human Use of Human Beings*, New York: Avon Books, 1954, p. 130.

19. Brian Swimme, *The Hidden Heart of the Cosmos*, New York: Orbis Books, 1996, p. 100.

20. The designation of modern humans as *Homo sapiens sapiens* is widespread; see, for example: Joseph Campbell, *Historical Atlas of World Mythology, Vol. I: The Way of the Animal Powers, Part 1: Mythologies of the Primitive Hunters and Gatherers*, New York: Harper & Row, Perennial Library, 1988, p. 22. Richard Leakey, *The Making of Mankind*, New York: E.P. Dutton, 1981, p. 18. Mary Maxwell, *Human Evolution: A Philosophical Anthropology*, New York: Columbia University Press, 1984, p. 294. John Pfeiffer, *The Creative Explosion: An Inquiry into the Origins of Art and Religion*, New York, Ithaca: Cornell University Press, 1982, p. 13. Clive Ponting, *A Green History of the World*, New York: Penguin Books, 1993, p. 28. In the popular press, see: *Newsweek* magazine, Nov. 10, 1986, p. 62, and Oct. 16, 1989, p. 71.

21. Freeman Dyson, *Infinite in All Directions*, New York: Harper & Row, 1988, p. 297.

22. Max Planck, *The Observer*, January 25, 1931.

23. Philip Cohen, "Can Protein Spring into Life?" in *New Scientist*, April 26, 1997, p. 18.

24. Mark Buchanan, "A Billion Brains Are Better Than One," in *New Scientist*, November 20, 2004.

25. Mitchel Resnick, "Changing the Centralized Mind," *Technology Review*, July 1994.

26. Greg Huang, "Tiny organisms remember the way," in *New Scientist*, March 17, 2007, p. 16.

27. Patrick Johnsson, "New Research Opens a Window on the Minds of Plants," *Christian Science Monitor*, March 3, 2005. "We now know there's an ability of self-recognition in plants, which is highly unusual and quite extraordinary that it's actually there," says Dr. Trewavas. "But why has no one come to grips with it? Because the prevailing view of a plant, even among plant biologists, is that it's a simple organism that grows reproducibly in a flower pot." Another study shows that plants appear to have the ability to communicate through the atmosphere. There is "tangible proof that plant-to-plant communication occurs on the ecosystem level," says the author of a study that discovered plants in a forest respond to stresses by producing significant amounts of a chemical form of aspirin. This results in the release of volatile organic compounds into the air that may help to activate an ecosystem-wide immune response to the stresses. See: "Plants in forest emit aspirin chemical to deal with stress: Discovery may help agriculture," *Science Daily*, September 25, 2008.

28. Donald Griffin, and Gayle Speck, "New Evidence of Animal Consciousness," in *Animal Cognition*, Vol. 7, No. 1, January 2004. Published by Springer. Also see, for example, Helen Phillips, "Known Unknowns," *New Scientist*, December 16, 2006.

29. See, for example, "Pigeons Show Superior Self-recognition Abilities to Three Year Old Humans," in *Science Daily* (www.sciencedaily.com), June 14, 2008. Also: "Six 'uniquely' human traits now found in animals," Kate Douglas, *New Scientist*, May 22, 2008.

30. Dean Radin, op. cit., p. 109. Also see: Harold Puthoff and Russell Targ, "A Perceptual Channel for Information Transfer over Kilometer Distances," published in the proceedings of the *I.E.E.E.* (vol. 64, no. 3), March 1976.

31. Radin, ibid., p. 144.

32. Russell Targ, Phyllis Cole, and Harold Puthoff, *Development of Techniques to Enhance Man/Machine Communication*, Stanford Research Institute, Menlo Park, California, prepared for NASA, contract 953653 Under NAS7-100, June 1974. Also see: Harold Puthoff and Russell Targ, op. cit., "A Perceptual Channel for Information Transfer over Kilometer Distances."

33. For example, Targ and Puthoff, "A Perceptual Channel," op. cit.

34. Harold Puthoff, "CIA-Initiated Remote Viewing At Stanford Research Institute," Institute for Advanced Studies at Austin, Texas, 1996. See: http://www.biomindsuperpowers.com/Pages/CIA-InitiatedRV.html.

35. Puthoff and Targ, op. cit., 338–40. Also see: R. Targ and H. Puthoff, *Mind-Reach: Scientists Look at Psychic Ability*, Delacorte Press/Eleaonor Friede, 1977.

36. Dean Radin, *Entangled Minds*, op. cit.

37. See, for example, professor Alexander Vilenkin of Tufts University, who has developed a model of the expanding universe that accounts for the birth of the universe "by quantum tunneling from nothing." "Birth of Inflationary Universes," in *Physical Review D*, 27:12 (1983), p. 2851. Other essays by Vilenkin: "Quantum Cosmology and the Initial State of the Universe, " in *Physical Review D*, 37 (1988), pp. 888–97, and "Approaches to Quantum Cosmology," in *Physical Review D*, 50 (1994), pp. 2581–94. Also see: the work of philosopher Quentin Smith, who writes in his essay "The Uncaused Beginning of the Universe" that: "...the most reasonable belief is that we came from nothing, by nothing and for nothing." William Lane Craig and Quentin Smith, *Theism, Atheism, and Big Bang Cosmology*, Oxford: Oxford University Press, 1993.

38. John Gribbin, *In the Beginning: The Birth of the Living Universe*, New York: Little, Brown, 1993, pp. 244–45. Also see: David Shiga, "Could black holes be portals to other universes?" *New Scientist*, April 27, 2007.

39. Ibid., p. 245.

40. Gregg Easterbrook, "What Came Before Creation?" in *U.S. News and World Report*, July 20, 1998, p. 48.

41. See, for example: Alex Vilenkin, *Many Worlds in One: The Search for Other Universes*, New York: Hill & Wang, 2006. Ervin Laszlo, *Science and the Akashic Field*, Rochester, VT: Inner Traditions, 2004. Primack and Abrams, op. cit.

42. Primack and Abrams, op. cit., p. 190.

Chapter 3

1. English translation provided by Jewish Publication Society, taken from http://www.sacred-texts.com/bib/jps/.

2. See, for example: *The Complete Biblical Library, The Old Testament, Hebrew-English Dictionary,* World Library Press, 1996.

3. Psalms 19:1, *New International Version*, International Bible Society, 1984.

4. For another point of view based upon the timeless nature of God's existence, see Psalm 19:2, "Text, Translation, and Notes," online at http://ancient hebrewpoetry.typepad.com/ancient_hebrew_poetry/2007/08/psalm-191-text-.html.

5. Psalms 139:7–10, *New International Version*, op. cit., 1984.

6. *New International Version*, ibid.

7. Matthew Fox, *Meditations with Meister Eckhart*, Santa Fe, New Mexico: Bear and Co., 1983, p. 24.

8. See: Ted Peters, *Cosmos as Creation*, Nashville: Abingdon Press, 1989, pp. 82–83.

9. It is important to differentiate between creationism and continuous creation because they differ in fundamental ways. *Creationism* focuses on a one-time event with no evolution, whereas *continuous creation* focuses on a continuous process that includes evolution as an integral aspect of its self-transforming dynamic. Creationism is a one-time event and thus static, whereas continuous creation sees the universe as dynamically regenerating itself and creatively unfolding through time.

10. A living-universe perspective brings new insight into the Last Supper where,

in a sacred ritual of remembrance, Jesus proclaimed that bread and wine were his body and blood. This makes literal sense when the universe is viewed as a living and continuously recreated entity: all things *are* the literal body of God—manifestations of a divine life force. Jesus could be providing a ritual for remembering that bread and wine are, both symbolically and literally, tangible expressions of a living universe and are infused with the sacred life force that sustains the entire universe.

11. See, for example, D. B. Macdonald, "Continuous recreation and atomic time in Muslim scholastic theology," *Isis* 9 (1927): 326–44; also, Majid Fakhry, *Islamic Occasionalism and Its Critique by Averroes and Aquinas*, London (1958). The Islamic view of occasionalism is more inclusive than the Western philosophy by the same name that was developed by the Cartesian school (which saw mind and body as absolutely separate; therefore, bodily motion was dependent on the co-operation of God).

12. Samuel Umen, *The World of the Mystic*, New York: Philosophical Library, 1988, p. 178.

13. See, for example, Coleman Barks, *The Essential Rumi*, San Francisco: HarperSanFrancisco, 1995.

14. A. H. Almaas, *The Inner Journey Home*, Boston: Shambhala, 2004.

15. Huston Smith, *The Religions of Mankind*, New York: Harper and Row, 1958, p. 73.

16. Sri Nisargadatta Majaraj, *I Am That*, Part I (trans. Maurice Frydman), Bombay, India: Chetana, 1973, p. 289.

17. Heinrich Zimmer, *Myths and Symbols in Indian Art and Civilization*, Joseph Campbell (ed.), Princeton, N.J.: Princeton University Press, Bollingen Series, 1972, p. 152.

18. Zimmer, ibid., p. 131.

19. Satprem, *Sri Aurobindo or the Adventure of Consciousness*, Pondicherry, India, 1970.

20. Swami Prabhavanada and Frederick Manchester, *The Upanishads: Breath of the Eternal*, New York: New American Library, 2002.

21. Ibid., p. 131.

22. Huston Smith, *The Religions of Man*, New York: Harper and Row, 1958.

23. *The Universe in a Single Atom: The Convergence of Science and Spirituality*, New York: Morgan Road Books, 2005, p. 81.

24. Govinda, *Creative Meditation and Multi-dimensional Consciousness*, Wheaton, IL: Theosophical Publishing House, 1976, p. 207.

25. Govinda, ibid., p. 9.

26. Namkhai Norbu, *The Crystal and the Way of Light: Sutra, Tantra, and Dzogchen* (compiled and edited by John Shane), New York: Routledge and Kegan Paul, 1986, p. 64.

27. D. T. Suzuki, *Zen and Japanese Culture*, Princeton, NJ: Princeton University Press, 1970, p. 364.

28. Ibid., p. 257.

29. Alan Watts, *The Middle Way: Journal of the Buddhist Society*, February 1973, London, p. 156.

30. Robert Linssen, *Living Zen*, New York: Grove Press, 1958.

31. Lao Tsu, *Tao Te Ching* (trans. Gia-Fu Feng and Jane English), New York: Vintage Books, 1972.

32. Mary Evelyn Tucker referenced in Samuel Snyder, "Chinese Traditions and Ecology," *Worldviews*, 2006.

33. Luther Standing Bear, quoted in Joseph Epes Brown, "Modes of Contemplation Through Actions: North American Indians," *Main Currents in Modern Thought,* New York: Center for Integrative Studies, November-December 1973, p. 194.

34. Malcolm Margolin, *The Ohlone Way: Indian Life in the San Francisco-Monterey Bay Area*, Berkeley: Heyday Books, 1978.

35. Ibid., pp. 142–43.

36. David Maybury-Lewis, *Millennium: Tribal Wisdom and the Modern World*, New York: Viking, 1992, pp. 197–202.

37. David Abram, *The Spell of the Sensuous*, New York: Vintage Books, 1996, p. 169.

38. Sam Keen, *Your Mythic Journey*, New York: Tarcher/Putnam Books, 1989, p. 90.

39. Richard Nelson, *Make Prayers to the Raven,* Chicago: University of Chicago Press, 1983, p. 14.

40. Plotinus, quoted in: John Gregory, *The Neo-Platonists,* Kyle Cathie, 1991, selected passages from the Enneads, 4.4.32.

41. Evelyn Underhill, *Mysticism*, New York: Meridian Books, 1955, p. 28.

42. Heraclitus, quoted in Timothy Ferris, *Galaxies*, New York: Stewart, Tabori and Chang, 1982, p. 87.

43. Alexander, "Space, Time and Deity," quoted in Underhill, op. cit., p. 29.

44. Bergson, ibid., p. 191.

Chapter 4

1. Thomas Berry, *The Dream of the Earth*, San Francisco: Sierra Club Books, 1988, p. 132.
2. Yervant Terzian and Elizabeth Bilson, eds., *Carl Sagan's Universe*, Cambridge University Press, 1997, p. 148. Also see the highly regarded physicist, Alex Vilenkin, who writes: "At the heart of the new worldview is the picture of an eternally inflating universe. It consists of isolated "island universes," where inflation has ended...." op. cit., p. 203. Also see, for example, Marcus Chown, "Into the Void," *New Scientist*, November 24, 2007, who explores whether a giant void in the universe could be the imprint of another universe.
3. Wheeler, quoted in Renee Weber, "The Good, the True, the Beautiful," in *Main Currents*, p. 139.
4. Ibid., p. 140.
5. Joseph Campbell, *The Power of Myth*, with Bill Moyers, New York: Doubleday, 1988, p. 217.
6. Stephen Mitchell (trans.), *Tao Te Ching: A New English Version*, Harper & Row, 1988, Chapter 25.
7. The quote by Shao is taken from: Garma Chang, *The Buddhist Teaching of Totality: The Philosophy of Hwa Yen Buddhism*, University Park: The Pennsylvania State University Press, 1971, p. 111.
8. Rumi, quoted in Andrew Harvey, *The Way of Passion: A Celebration of Rumi*, Berkeley: Frog, Ltd., 1994, p.189.
9. Yung-chia Hsuan-chueh was a scholar and a monk who lived in the years 665 to 713 and was one of the most gifted teachers of the Ch'an (Zen) school during the T'ang Dynasty of China.
10. *Lankavatara Sutra*, D. T. Suzuki, trans., Boulder: Prajña Press, 1978, p. 8.
11. Underhill, *Mysticism*, op. cit., p. 101.

Chapter 5

1. Brian Swimme, op. cit., p. 112.
2. Russell Targ was the co-founder of the psychic research program at SRI in the early 1970s and would later write, "We are not a body, but rather *limitless, nonlocal awareness* animating or residing as a body." [emphasis in original] See: Targ, *Limitless Mind: A Guide to Remote Viewing and Transformation of Consciousness*, Novato: CA: New World Library, 2004, p. xii.
3. Bernard Haisch, *The God Theory*, op. cit.

4. David Bohm, op. cit., p. 45.

5. James Robinson, ed., *Nag Hammadi Library*, 1st edition, San Francisco: Harper & Row, 1977, p. 123. Elsewhere in the Gnostic sources, Jesus is quoted by the disciple James as saying: "Search ever and cease not till ye find the mysteries of the Light, which will lead you into the Light-kingdom."

6. See, for example, the article: "The Quakers: Children of the Light," at the Quaker site: http://www.fum.org/about/friends.htm Also see a discussion of inward light at: http://www.quakers.org/inwardlight.php

7. Robert Cummings Neville (ed.), *Ultimate Realities*, New York: SUNY, 2001, p. 52.

8. See, for example: Llewellyn Vaughan-Lee, *Alchemy of Light*, Inverness, CA: Golden Sufi Center, 2007.

9. Quoted in Andrew Harvey, *The Way of Passion*, op. cit., p.138.

10. Most Buddhists do not deny the existence of a soul as a life stream of luminous consciousness; instead, they deny the soul is an unchanging, autonomous entity. In turn, meditation is seen as a vehicle for discovering ourselves as an ever-flowing life stream and relaxing directly into the flow of self-luminous knowing.

11. Harvey, ibid., p. 160.

12. Robert Bly (trans.), *The Kabir Book*, Boston: Beacon Press, 1977, p. 21.

13. "Love" is described in the *Encyclopedia of Religion*, 2nd edition, Woodbridge, CT: Macmillan Reference, December 2004.

14. Quoted in Matthew Fox, *Creation Spirituality*, op. cit., p. 28.

15. Ibn al-Arabi, quoted in Robert Ellwood, Jr., *Mysticism and Religion*, New Jersey: Prentice-Hall, 1980, p. 92.

16. Jesus quoted in The Gospel of Thomas, Nag Hammadi Library, James Robertson, general editor, San Francisco: Harper & Row, 1977, p. 124.

17. An Arabic inscription on a city gate of Fatepuhr-Sikri in India.

18. See, for example, Tsele Natsok Rangdrol, *The Mirror of Mindfulness: The Cycle of the Four Bardos*, E. Kunsang (trans.), Boston: Shambhala Press, 1989.

19. Rangdrol, Ibid., pp. 8–10.

20. HH the XIV Dalai Lama, *The Heart of Compassion: A Practical Approach to a Meaningful Life*, Wisconsin: Lotus Press, 2002.

21. Robert Bly (trans.), op. cit., p. 24.

Chapter 6

1. Scientists are now expanding their description of "life" in recognition there may be life forms thriving on another planet but living in a sea of liquid methane instead of water or living on hydrochloric acid instead of energy from the sun. See, for example, Douglas Fox, "Life in the Deep Freeze," *New Scientist*, August 12, 2006, p. 35. Bacteria have been found buried kilometers deep in the ice sheets of Antarctica and Greenland, with temperatures as low as –40 degrees centigrade, living for hundreds of thousands of years in a film of water at little as three molecules thick.

2. There are complex, self-organizing processes going on even at the scale of entire galaxies. Our Milky Way galaxy, with its several hundred billion stars, had been assumed to be no more than a simple, whirling disk of matter. Now, our galaxy is being described by scientists as a "dynamic, living object" that is "breathing—pushing out gas and then pulling it back in, as if exhaling and inhaling." (See: Bart P. Wakker and Philipp Richte, "Our Growing, Breathing Galaxy," *Scientific American*, January 2004.) Our enormous galaxy is a complex ecological system that is nurturing star systems that are in turn producing planets that grow our forms of life. Galaxies are cosmic gardens comprised of billions of stars in a complex, ongoing partnership with streaming gases and energy, all necessary to create the conditions for growing a rich diversity of life within a galaxy.

3. See: Note 20 in Chapter 2, page 208.

4. Tsele Natsok Rangdrol, Erik Pema Kunsang, trans., *The Mirror of Mindfulness: The Cycle of the Four Bardos*, Boston: Shambhala, 1989, pps. 10–11.

Chapter 7

1. Joseph Campbell, *The Hero with a Thousand Faces*, New York: Meridian Book Edition, 1956, p. 30.

2. See Chapter 2 of Elgin, *Awakening Earth*, New York: William Morrow, 1993.

3. See: http://www-geology.ucdavis.edu/~GEL134/ambrose.pdf.

4. For a more extensive exploration of driving trends, see Elgin, *Promise Ahead*, op. cit., Chapter 2: "Adversity Trends: Hitting an Evolutionary Wall."

5. Robert Bly (trans.), op. cit., p. 11.

6. See: Karen Thompson, *The Great Transformation*, New York: Knopf, 2006.

7. D. H. Lawrence, *Apocalypse,* 1931.

8. These three stages are explored in depth in Elgin, *Awakening Earth*, op. cit., Chapters 5, 6, 7.

9. See, for example, Chang, *The Buddhist Teaching of Totality*, op. cit., p. 39.

10. It is important to differentiate the flow consciousness described here from the far more restricted definition of flow experience described by Mihaly Csikszenthmihalyi in his book, *Flow: The Psychology of Optimal Experience*, New York: Harper & Row, 1990.

Chapter 8

1. Mihail Nimay, *Book of Mirdad*, Baltimore: Penguin Books, 1971.

2. Quoted in: Stephen Oates, *Let the Trumpets Sound: The Life of Martin Luther King, Jr.*, New York: New American Library, 1982, p. 226.

3. Pitirim Sorokin, *The Ways and Power of Love*, Chicago: Henry Regnery, 1967 (orig. 1954), p. 71.

4. This description is drawn primarily from: Sorokin, op. cit., p. 67, and Eknath Easwaran, *The Compassionate Universe*, Petaluma, CA: Nilgiri Press, 1989.

5. Gitanjali Kolanad, *Culture Shock! India,* Portland, OR: Graphic Arts Center Publishing, 1994, p. 23.

6. Ibid., p. 69.

7. Arnold Toynbee, *A Study of History* (abridgement of Vol's I–VI, by D. C. Somerville), New York: Oxford University Press, 1947, p. 198.

Chapter 9

1. Another useful resource for appreciating a sense of the human scale: Go on-line and look for "powers of ten" videos; they provide a fascinating look into the realms of the very large and the very small relative to the human scale.

2. See Chapter 1 of Elgin, *Promise Ahead*, op. cit., "Is Humanity Growing Up?"

Index

Koyukon Indians (Alaska), central
beliefs, 77

Lakota (middle western U.S.), view of
the universe, 76
Lanbkavatara Sutra, Zen wisdom
traditions, 88
language, animal use of, 46
Last Supper, ritual of the, 211–212
Laszlo, Ervin, reality of the quantum
vacuum, 85
Law of Progressive Simplification
(Toynbee), 173
Lawrence, D.H., on the first axial age,
144
life
compassion for life, 167
connection between mindfulness and
concentration, 150
necessary relationships for existence of,
27
life force, foundation of existence,
117–119
life forms, alien, 215–216
lifestyles
changing to earth-friendly, 176
of simplicity, 172–176
light, nature of, 98–102
Linssen, Robert, a skilled meditator's
view of the world, 73
living, sustainable, 175, 178
Living One, recognizing the, 111
location, where are we, 2
logic, whole systems of a "living
universe," 55
love
and awareness, 105–108
impact and enduring power of, 170–
172
Luthr Standing Bear, Lakota teachings,
76

Majarj, Sri Nisargadatta, your existence
in the universe, 69
mass media, the collective mirror of,
179–184

Master Universe. *See* Mother Universe
matter
dark, 22–24, 202
designing, 28
maturity, testing our, 143
meditation
Buddhist, 72–73
experiencing flow, 108
feedback and, 48–49
practicing intense, 5
meditations
on becoming beings of light, 194
on building a universe, 190
with conscious aliveness, 192–193
on knowing, 194
on living in harmony with others, 194
looking into space, 191–192
on love, 194
on our invisible self, 191
practing flow consciousness, 193
reality surfing, 193
with reflective consciousness, 192
visualizing ourselves as giants, 190–191
Merton, Thomas, impact of life events
on the soul, 113
Meta-Universe. *See* Mother Universe
mindfulness, balance between
concentration and, 150
mindsets, evolving, 6–7
miracles, American Indian lore's three,
19
mirror
of consciousness, 148
mass media as an effective social,
179–184
Mitchell, Edgar, observing the entire
universe from space, 11
mold, slime, 44–45
molecules, primary perception of, 44
Mother Universe
description of God, 86
existence of a, 54
key attributes of, 89–90
superspace, 85
movements, retrofitting for a sustainable
future, 177

About the Author

DUANE ELGIN is an internationally recognized visionary, speaker, and author. He earned his MBA from the Wharton Business School and then an MA in economic history from the University of Pennsylvania. In 2001 he was awarded an honorary PhD for work in "ecological and spiritual transformation" from the California Institute of Integral Studies in San Francisco. In 2006 Elgin received the Goi International Peace Award in recognition of his contribution to a global "vision, consciousness, and lifestyle" that fosters a "more sustainable and spiritual culture."

In the early 1970s Elgin worked in Washington, D.C., as a senior staff member of a joint Presidential-Congressional Commission on the American Future. He then moved to California to work as a senior social scientist with the think tank SRI International, where he co-authored numerous studies on the long-range future. With Joseph Campbell and a small team of scholars, he co-authored the report that later became the book *Changing Images of Man* (1982). He co-authored other major reports as well: *Anticipating Future National and Global Problems* (for the President's Science Advisor), *Alternative Futures for Environmental Policy* (for the Environmental Protection Agency), and *Limits to the Management of Large, Complex Systems* (for the National Science Foundation).

Seeing the challenges ahead, Elgin left SRI in 1977 to focus on writing and non-partisan organizing of citizens around issues of media accountability and citizen empowerment. Elgin's first book was published in 1981: *Voluntary Simplicity: Toward a Way of Life That Is Outwardly Simple, Inwardly Rich* (3rd edition, forthcoming). This pioneering book is recognized as a classic in exploring more sustainable and meaningful ways of living. The idea of a living universe was at the foundation of his next book, *Awakening Earth: Exploring the Evolution of Human Culture and Consciousness* (1993). This is a big-picture overview of the evolution of human consciousness, both personal and social, from awakening hunter-gatherers to the modern era and then into the deep future. Elgin's third book, *Promise Ahead: A Vision of Hope and Action for Humanity's Future* (2000), explored the "adversity trends" and the "opportunity trends" that were converging at that time; it suggested ways the human family could avoid an evolutionary crash and instead realize an evolutionary leap forward. Elgin has also contributed chapters to sixteen books, and published more than seventy articles on subjects ranging from social transformation and simplicity to media accountability and a living universe.

Elgin has been researching the theme of a living universe for the past twenty-seven years, and elements of his work have been published in scholarly journals. In 1988 he published the lengthy article on the cosmology of a reflective and regenerative universe:

"The Living Cosmos: A Theory of Continuous Creation," for the journal *Revision*. His article, "The Paradigm of a Living Universe," was published in the *Journal of World Futures* (2000) and presents a scholarly summary of his cosmology. Two of his books—*Awakening Earth* and *Promise Ahead*—included chapters on the theme of a living cosmos. *The Living Universe* brings these years of inquiry together for the first time.

In addition to decades of scholarship, Elgin also brings forty years of meditation and inner inquiry to his exploration of a living universe. He has been inspired by all of the world's wisdom traditions, especially Buddhist, Quaker, Gnostic Christian, and Hindu. Elgin has also had extensive experience with psychic research in a scientific setting. For nearly three years in the early 1970s he was one of four primary subjects who participated in numerous experiments funded by the National Aeronautics and Space Administration to explore our intuitive potentials. These experiments were conducted at SRI International, where Elgin worked doing futures research. Results from these experiments (notably, remote viewing) have been published in major scientific journals. A portion of Elgin's work is described in the scientific paper by Puthoff and Targ, "A Perceptual Channel for Information Transfer over Kilometer Distances," published in the proceedings of the prestigious I.E.E.E. (1976). His work is also described in their book *MindReach: Scientists Look at Psychic Ability* (1977).

As a speaker, Elgin has given more than 250 keynotes and workshops with audiences ranging from business executives and civic groups to college students and religious organizations. Common topics are "the world at the tipping point," "sustainable and meaningful ways of living," "the living universe," and "four archetypes for imagining a promising future." A series of online courses is available through his website. Elgin has also co-produced short streaming videos for the Internet that look at key aspects of the human journey. His videos, courses and extensive writing are available on his website:

www.awakeningearth.org